learn

Windows 98

Stephen C. Solosky

Ken Baldauf

que
E&T

Learn Windows 98

Library of Congress Catalog No: 98-89905

ISBN: 1-58076-001-5

Screens reproduced in this book were created using Collage Plus from Inner Media, Inc., Hollis, NH.

Credits

Publisher
Robert Linsky

Executive Editor
Jon Phillips

Series Editors
Robert L. Ferrett
John Preston
Sally Preston

Director of Product Marketing
Susan L. Kindel

Operations Manager
Christine Moos

Software Coordinator
Angela Denny

Team Coordinator
Melody Layne

Designer
Louisa Klucznik

Copy Editors
Cynthia Fields
Theresa Wehrle

Layout
Louis Porter, Jr.

Indexer
Becky Hornyak

About the Authors

Ken Baldauf heads up the Computer Literacy program at Florida State University in Tallahassee, Florida. His Bachelor's degree is in Music Theory and his Master's degree in Computer Science. Ken's been an active teacher for over twenty years, teaching music through the first portion of his life and computers for the second. His current position at FSU involves managing thousands of computer literacy students and teachers each semester and lecturing on computer concepts, object-oriented programming, Internet applications, and Web authoring. Ken has authored several titles for Macmillan Publishing, including *Windows NT4 Essentials*, *Windows 98 Essentials*, and *Learn Windows NT4*.

Stephen C. Solosky is a Professor of Mathematics/ Statistics/Computer Processing at Nassau Community College, Garden City, New York. He holds a B.S. from Old Dominion University and an M.B.A. from New York Institute of Technology. He is the author of *Visual Basic 5 Smart Start* and has written other books on computer programming and database processing. He has extensive experience in developing computer applications for business and industry, as well as in the design and presentation of computer training programs for various organizations.

Trademark Acknowledgments

Philosophy of the Learn Series

The Learn Series has been designed for students who need to master the basics of a particular software program quickly. The books are visual in nature to help students master the basics easily. Steps are accompanied by figures that show the results of the steps. Visual cues are given in the form of highlights and callouts to help direct students to the location in the window that is being used in a particular step. Explanatory text is minimized in the actual steps but is included when appropriate in additional pedagogical elements. Every lesson includes reinforcement exercises to give students a chance to practice their skills immediately.

Structure of a Learn Series Book

Each of the books in the Learn series is structured in the same way for the sake of consistency. The following elements are included in each book.

Introduction

Each book has an introduction designed to provide students with an overview of what they will be learning. This consists of an introduction to the series (how to use this book), a brief introduction to the Windows 98 operating system (if appropriate), and an introduction to the software.

Lesson Introduction

The introduction to each lesson includes the lesson number and title and a brief introduction to the topics covered in the lesson.

Task Introduction

All tasks included in the lesson are listed on the opening page of each lesson to give students a road map. Each task is explained in a section at the beginning of the task.

Completed Project

A screen capture or printout of the results of each lesson is included at the beginning of the lesson to provide an example of what is accomplished in the lesson.

"Why would I do this?"

At the beginning of each task is a "Why would I do this?" section, which is a short explanation of the relevance of the task. This section illustrates why a particular element of the software is important and how it can be used effectively.

Figures

Steps have accompanying figures, which are placed to the right or left of the steps. The figures show what the result of the steps will be. Figures provide the reader with visual reinforcement of the task at hand, and also highlight buttons, menu choices, and other screen elements used in the task.

Pedagogical Elements

Three recurring elements are found in the Preston Ferrett Learn series:

 In Depth: detailed look at a topic or procedure, or another way of doing something.

 Quick Tip: faster or more efficient way of doing something.

 Pothole: area where trouble may be encountered, along with instructions on how to recover from and/or avoid these mistakes.

Glossary

New words or concepts are printed in *italic* the first time they are presented. Definitions of these words or phrases are included in the glossary at the back of the book.

End-of-Lesson Material

The end-of-lesson material includes Student and Application Exercises. The Student Exercises consist of the following:

True/False questions. Ten True/False questions enable students to test their understanding of the new material in the lesson.

Visual Identification. A captured screen or screens offer students the opportunity to test their familiarity with various screen elements introduced in the lesson.

Matching. Ten Matching questions are included to give students a chance to assess their familiarity with concepts and procedures introduced in the lesson.

Application Exercises. Included at the end of each lesson, these consist of three to five exercises that provide practice in the skills introduced in the tasks. These exercises generally follow the sequence of the tasks in the lesson. Each exercise usually builds on the previous exercise, so it is a good idea to do them in the order in which they are presented.

Student Data Files

To access the student data files that accompany this book, insert the *Learn Windows 98* CD-ROM and click on the CD-ROM drive in Windows Explorer or My Computer. To open the graphics file called **Circles**, for example, follow these steps:

1 Right-click the CD-ROM drive from Windows Explorer. A shortcut menu will appear. *Note:* If you have just inserted the CD-ROM, you can click on **Browse** from the Autorun screen, which will open Windows Explorer to the CD-ROM drive; then you can proceed with step 3.

2 Click **Open.** The contents of the CD-ROM will appear in the window.

3 Double-click on the **Student** folder. The available student data files will appear in the **Student** window.

4 Double-click on the **Circles** file. Microsoft Paint will launch and the **Circles** file will open.

 In Depth: The student data files may also be installed on the computer's hard drive or on a network. To install the files to the hard drive (check with your instructor first), see "Working with the Files from the CD-ROM" later in this preface.

Annotated Instructor's Manual

If you have adopted this text for use in a college classroom, you will receive, upon request, an Annotated Instructor's Manual (AIM) at no additional charge. The Annotated Instructor's Manual is a comprehensive teaching tool that contains the student text with margin notes and tips for instructors and students. The AIM also contains suggested curriculum guides for courses of varying lengths, answers to the end-of-chapter material, test questions and answers, and PowerPoint slides. Data files and solutions for each tutorial and exercise, along with a PowerPoint presentation, are included on disc with the AIM. Please contact your local representative or write to us on school or business letterhead at Prentice Hall, 1 Lake Street, Upper Saddle River, New Jersey, 07458.

Introduction to Windows 98

In 1985, Microsoft introduced its first version of Windows to make the personal computer (PC) easier to use. The Windows environment relies on graphics, rather than commands, to communicate with users. In a graphical environment, easy-to-understand pictures are used to represent programs, procedures, and files. When you want to direct the computer to perform a task, you click or select a picture, rather than use a technical command.

Prior to the introduction of Windows, PC owners had to learn or look up cumbersome text commands to perform the simplest of functions. In the old text environment, PC users memorized the commands they used most often to save time. Each command was different, and many were quite complex. Using a PC before the introduction of Windows was definitely a more laborious experience.

The term used to describe the newer, easier, graphical Windows environment is graphical user interface, or GUI (pronounced "gooey") for short. In 1995, Microsoft introduced (with great fanfare!) a new version with the most powerful graphical user interface ever—Windows 95. There are two primary benefits of a GUI system. The most obvious benefit is that a graphical user interface makes the personal computer easier to use. Pictures are easier to follow than memorizing keyboard commands. A second benefit of a GUI is that it provides a consistent way to work within a program, with other programs, and to switch between programs. Because a GUI provides one consistent interface, once you learn the procedures for running one program, you can run any Windows or Windows-compatible program without much new learning.

Windows 98 is also an operating system or systems software. It is the system used to give your computer instructions needed to operate the computer. Another operating system with which you are most likely familiar, and to which you will be introduced briefly in this book, is DOS (Disk Operating System). Prior versions of Windows used DOS as their operating system. Windows 3.1 was the first version of Windows that simplified the use of DOS. With Windows 3.1, users no longer had to memorize DOS commands, because DOS performed tasks in the background that users were unaware of. The introduction of Windows 95 changed everything because it replaced DOS as the operating system. Why, you might ask, does this book introduce the concept of DOS at all? Because older

hardware and some software programs still use DOS to run. In this book, you will learn how to open the DOS Prompt window and familiarize yourself with some basic DOS commands in the event that you must work with a DOS-based application.

There are thousands of software application programs that you can purchase to run on your Windows 98 operating system, such as Microsoft's Word, Access, Excel, and PowerPoint. Others include WordPerfect, Lotus 1-2-3, and CorelDraw. When you purchase Windows 98, Microsoft provides some of its own basic, simple software applications, including WordPad and Paint, which you will use in this book.

The Concept of This Book

This book is designed for students who are new to Windows 98 and would like to know how to use it in real-life applications. The author and series editors have combined their many years of business experience and classroom teaching to provide a basic step-by-step approach that leads to the development of skills advanced enough to be useful in the workplace. We have designed the book so that you will be successful immediately and will learn important basics in the first lesson. In the lessons that follow, you will learn how to work with menus and dialog boxes, work with folders and files, control applications, get help, use handy Windows accessories, share data between windows, and personalize your Windows 98 settings.

Working with the Files from the CD-ROM

If you are working on a computer in a lab, verify that you can save the files to the hard drive. Some schools and universities do not allow you to save files to the computers in the computer labs. If the files have been installed on a network or by a lab assistant, your instructor will inform you where the files are located.

After inserting the CD-ROM, an installation screen will appear. The screen has three options:

- Install—This option allows you to install the student data files that accompany the text.

- Browse—This option opens Windows Explorer and displays the contents of the CD-ROM. This is one option you can use to access the student data files directly from the CD-ROM.

- Exit—This option closes the installation window and returns you to the Windows desktop.

Installing the Files to Your Hard Drive

If you have been instructed to install the files on a lab computer or if you are installing them on your home computer, follow these steps:

1 From the installation screen, click the **Install** button.

2 The Welcome dialog box is displayed. Click the **Next** button.

3 The Readme.txt appears. The Readme.txt gives you important information regarding the installation. Make sure you use the scrollbar to view the entire Readme.txt file. When you are finished reading the Readme.txt, click the **Next** button.

4 The Select Destination Directory is displayed. Unless instructed otherwise by your instructor, the default location is recommended. Click **Next**.

5 The Ready to Install screen appears. Click **Next** to begin the installation.

A directory will be created on your hard drive where the student files will be installed. The installation of the student data files allows you to access the data files from the Start menu programs. To access the student data files from the Start menu, click **Start**, click **Programs**, and then click **Learn Windows 98**. The student data files are located in the Student folder.

6 A dialog box appears confirming that the installation is complete.

Uninstalling the Student Data Files

There is also a program to uninstall the student data files. The following steps walk you through the process:

1 Click on the **Start** button and then click **Programs**.

2 Click **Learn Windows 98**.

3 Click **Uninstall Learn Windows 98**.

4 Click one of the Uninstall methods listed:

- Automatic—This method deletes all files in the directory and all shortcuts created.

- Custom—This method allows you to select the files you want to delete.

5 Click **Next**.

6 The Perform Uninstall dialog box appears. Click **Finish**. The Student data files and directories will be deleted.

Table of Contents

Lesson 1
The Basics

Introduction

This lesson is designed to provide you with the basic skills needed to use Windows 98. In this lesson, you learn how to start Windows 98, use the mouse, work within the Windows GUI (graphical user interface), and, finally, shut down Windows 98.

Visual Summary

When you are done with Task 3, you will have a Windows 98 desktop that looks like this:

Task 1

Using the Mouse

Why would I do this?

Windows presents information in a visual way so you can easily access what you need without having to memorize numerous commands and keystrokes. To use Windows 98 effectively, you need to learn how to use the mouse. The *mouse* is a "pointing device" that has two or more buttons and connects to the computer.

In this task, you learn how to manipulate different Windows 98 elements by moving the mouse on the mousepad and by pressing the left mouse button.

My Computer icon   Mouse pointer

1 Turn on your computer and wait for Windows 98 to load. Move the mouse on your mousepad until the tip of the mouse pointer rests on the picture labeled My Computer on the computer screen. This action is called *pointing*. Onscreen objects (such as the one labeled My Computer) are called *icons*.

Pothole: Startup instructions may vary from computer to computer depending on whether you are using a standalone computer, a network, or certain login procedures.

Quick Tip: In Windows 98, the computer screen is frequently referred to as the *desktop*.

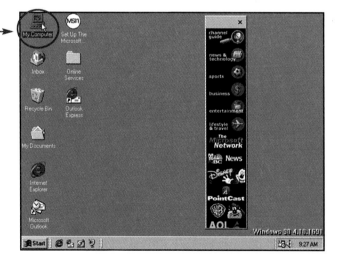

2 Press and release the left mouse button on the **My Computer** icon to select it. The selected object displays in a different color or in reverse video. Quickly pressing and releasing the left mouse button is called *clicking*.

Quick Tip: Rest the heel of your hand on the surface of the mousepad or desk when using the mouse. This will ensure steady control when you click or move the mouse.

3 Press the left mouse button again while pointing to the **My Computer** icon, but this time don't release it. While holding down the left mouse button, move the mouse across the mousepad. This action is called *dragging*. As you drag, notice a "ghost" of the icon moves with the mouse pointer onscreen. Release the mouse button, and the icon "drops" to another position. (Note: Move the **My Computer** icon back to its original position by dragging and dropping the icon with the mouse.)

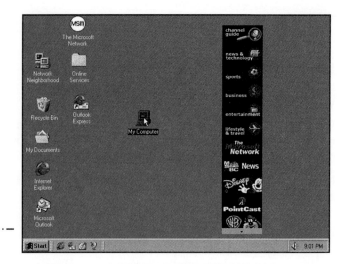

Double-click an icon to open the window it represents.

Pothole: Windows 98 can be configured with a "single click" option. If Windows 98 "single click" option is selected, you only need to place your mouse over an object to select it and single-click objects to open them.

4 Point to the **My Computer** icon and quickly press and release the left mouse button twice. This action is called *double-clicking*. The My Computer icon opens the window it represents. You double-click icons and folders in Windows 98 to open a window, program, drive, or document.

Pothole: The My Computer window on your computer may look quite different than the one in the figure. This could be due to your window size of folder option settings. Check with your instructor.

5 Click the **Close** button in the upper-right corner of the My Computer window to close it.

Task 2

Using the Start Button

Why would I do this?

The taskbar is located on the bottom of the Windows 98 screen. On the left side of the taskbar is the Start button. It enables you to run applications, re-open documents, customize Windows settings, get help, and more. You use the Start button to initiate many of the tasks you will perform in Windows.

In this task, you learn how to use the Start button.

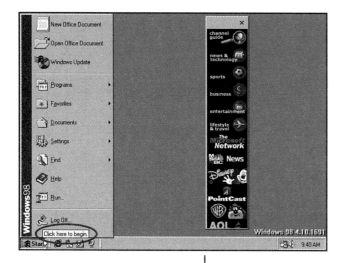

1 Point to the **Start** button on the taskbar with the mouse pointer. Leave the pointer motionless on the Start button for a moment. A helpful ScreenTip is displayed, which reads, "Click here to begin." Now, click the left mouse button and the Start menu will appear.

In Depth: A *ScreenTip* is a small box containing the name or some information about the object to which you are pointing.

2 Move the mouse pointer to the **Programs** command. As you point to the **Programs** command, a submenu "cascades" out, showing the list of programs available on your computer. This list displays a submenu of programs (in alphabetical order). For example, the Programs menu item may contain such Windows programs as Microsoft Word or Windows Explorer.

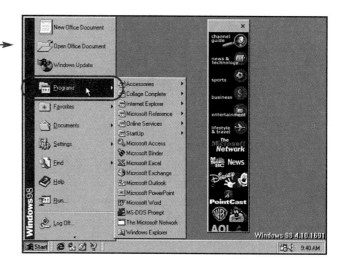

Pothole: Depending on your computer's configuration, your program list may contain many other programs that are not shown in the figure.

Quick Tip: Whenever you are asked to click an object, the left mouse button is implied. If you are expected to click the right mouse button, you will be asked to right-click the object.

3 Point to the **Accessories** command to reveal a submenu of programs for this selection. If you want to start a program on the submenu, point to the program name and click. For now, click any area of the desktop where there is not an object, and all of the menus will close.

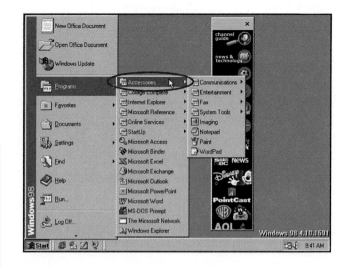

In Depth: You may be wondering about the *channel bar*, the other object conspicuously placed on the Windows 98 desktop. It gives you quick access to your favorite sites and the most popular Web content (like The Microsoft Network, MSNBC News, and Disney) on the Internet. The channel bar and the Internet will be discussed in more detail in Lesson 8.

Task 3

Opening a Window

Why would I do this?

Windows 98 displays all of its information in onscreen boxes called *windows*. Before you can work with any of the information on your computer, you must know how to display (or open) these windows. In a previous task, you opened the My Computer window by double-clicking its icon.

In this task, you learn how to use an alternative method of opening windows: a shortcut menu.

1 Point to the **My Computer** icon with the mouse pointer.

2 Right-click the **My Computer** icon to display the shortcut menu.

Quick Tip: By right-clicking the mouse button on some objects, you can open their *shortcut menus*. Try right-clicking when the mouse pointer is on the taskbar to see the shortcut menu for the taskbar.

3 Click the word **Open** with the left mouse button to choose that command. The My Computer window opens. Note that the button for the My Computer window is displayed on the taskbar next to the Start button.

Task 4

Minimizing and Maximizing a Window

Why would I do this?

You can reduce (minimize) or enlarge (maximize) program and document windows to organize your desktop and make working with your PC easier. You would minimize a window to move it out of your way temporarily, while leaving it active for later use. You would maximize a window so that you can see more of its contents onscreen.

In this task, you learn how to minimize, maximize, and restore a window.

1 With the My Computer window open, place the mouse pointer on the **Minimize** button, as shown in the figure. Click the left mouse button. The My Computer window minimizes and its button on the taskbar looks raised instead of recessed.

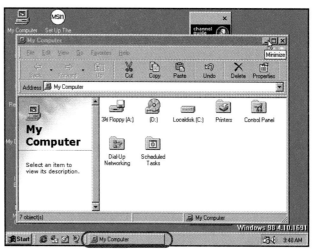

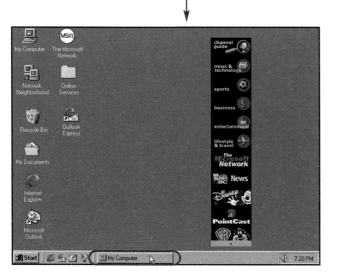

2 Click the **My Computer** button on the taskbar. The My Computer window opens.

3 Click the **Maximize** button in the upper-right corner of the My Computer window. The window expands to fill the desktop and the Maximize button changes to the **Restore** button.

Restore button

4 Click the **Restore** button on the window to change the window back to its former size.

Quick Tip: The minimize, maximize or restore, and close buttons are located on the *title bar* of a window. Also located on the title bar of a window is the name (title) of the window and its icon.

Task 5

Moving and Sizing a Window

Why would I do this?

As you add more applications, folders, and shortcuts to your desktop, you will need more room to display these elements. You can resize a window to save room on the desktop and move the windows so you can see all the open windows at one time.

In this task, you learn how to move and size windows.

Title bar

1 At the top of a window is the *title bar*. It includes the title of the open window and icons for maximizing or restoring, minimizing, and closing the window. Place the mouse pointer in the middle of the **My Computer** title bar. Hold down the left mouse button and drag the window to a new position on the desktop. The window moves with the mouse pointer. When the button is released, the window and its contents are "dropped" at the new location.

Quick Tip: Unless otherwise indicated, you will use the left mouse button to click, drag, or size windows.

2 Position the mouse pointer on the left border of the **My Computer** window. Its shape changes to a double-headed arrow.

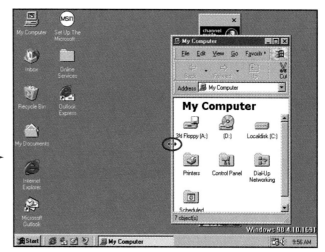

3 Click and drag the **double-headed arrow** to the right then release the mouse button. The window contracts when you release the mouse button.

4 Click and drag the double-headed arrow to the left, then release the mouse button. The window expands.

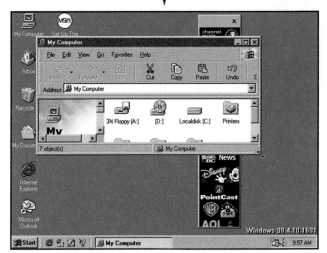

5 Click and drag the lower-right corner of the window to resize both dimensions at one time. You can drag any corner of a window.

Vertical scrollbar

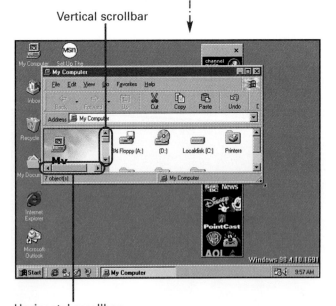

Horizontal scrollbar

6 If a window is too small to show all of its contents, horizontal and/or vertical scrollbars are displayed. Click the **arrow** at either end of a scrollbar on the My Computer window to view the hidden contents of the window. Scrolling lets you see all of a window's contents.

Quick Tip: To use a scrollbar, click the arrow at one end of the scrollbar, click and drag the scrollbar box, or click anywhere along the scrollbar.

Task 6

Closing Windows

Why would I do this?

You will want to close a window when you are finished working with it and its contents. Too many open windows clutter your desktop, as well as the taskbar.

In this task, you learn how to close a window.

1 To close the **My Computer** window, click the **Close** button in the upper-right corner of the window's title bar.

Quick Tip: As a shortcut to close a window, select the window and press (Alt)+(F4). Another alternative is to double-click the Control menu box, which is the icon located in the upper-left corner of the window's title bar. Another method of closing a window is to pull down the **File** menu by clicking the word File beneath the title bar and then choosing the **Close** command.

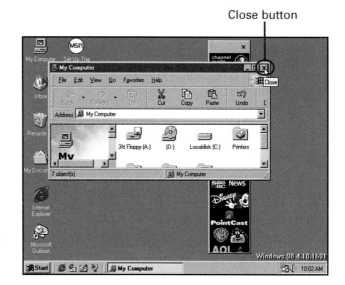

Close button

Task 7

Shutting Down the Computer

Why would I do this?

If you turn off the power to your computer before you shut it down, you could lose valuable data or damage an open file. Windows provides a safe Shut Down which properly prepares the computer to shut down in an orderly manner and reminds you if you forgot to save your work.

In this task, you learn how to shut down your computer.

1 Click the **Start** button on the taskbar and then click **Shut Down**. Windows checks the system and prepares for the shut down.

> **Quick Tip:** It is a good idea to close all open windows before you shut down your computer.

> **In Depth:** If your computer is connected to a network, you might not want to completely shut down. You may wish to simply close your work session and allow another user to begin. To do so, you would choose "Log off" from the Start menu rather than "shut down."

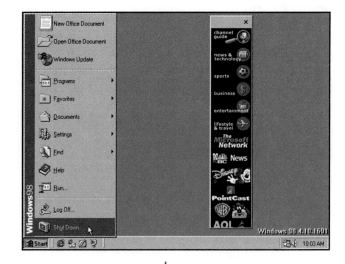

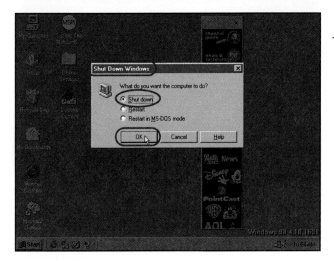

2 The **Shut Down Windows** dialog box opens. The option button next to the Shut down option is selected. This is called the default selection. Click the **OK** button to shut down your computer. Windows displays a final screen that tells you when it is safe to turn off the power to your computer.

> **In Depth:** When you need to work from DOS only instead of Windows, Windows 98 provides an easy way to boot to DOS. When you choose **Shut Down** from the **Start** menu, the Shut Down Windows dialog box opens. Choose the **Restart in MS-DOS** mode option button, and then click **OK**.

Student Exercises

True-False

For each of the following, circle either T or F to indicate whether the statement is true or false.

T   F   **1.** To select an object, using the mouse, place the mouse pointer on the object and click the left mouse button.

T   F   **2.** An object's context-sensitive, shortcut menu can be accessed by double-clicking the object.

T   F   **3.** Double-clicking a desktop icon will open the icon's associated program in a window.

T   F   **4.** All Windows' programs run in their own window on the desktop.

T   F   **5.** To maximize a window is to enlarge the font size.

T   F   **6.** Minimizing a window has the same effect as closing it.

T   F   **7.** When you wish to temporarily leave an application, it's best to click the window's close button.

T   F   **8.** Windows 98 allows for more than one application window to be open at a time.

T   F   **9.** A window has three size options: minimized, maximized, and mediumized.

T   F   **10.** You end your work session on Windows 98 by clicking the Start button.

Identifying Parts of the Windows 98 Screen

Refer to the figure and identify the numbered parts of the screen. Write the letter of the correct label in the space next to the number.

1. _____
2. _____
3. _____
4. _____
5. _____
6. _____
7. _____
8. _____
9. _____

A. Icon

B. Window

C. Title bar

D. Taskbar

E. Desktop

F. Mouse pointer

G. Maximize

H. Close

I. Minimize

J. Start

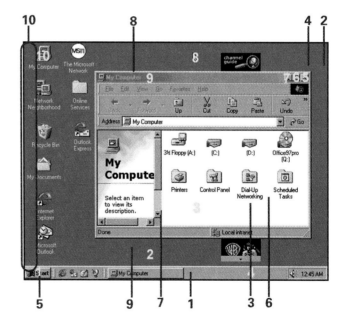

Matching

Match the statements below to the word or phrase that is the best match from the list. Write the letter of the matching word or phrase in the space provided next to the number.

1. ___ The place at which most tasks begin.

2. ___ Click this button when you wish to temporarily leave a program.

3. ___ This type of menu is revealed when you click the right mouse button on an icon.

4. ___ Look here to find the Start button.

5. ___ A small box containing the name or some information about an object being pointed to.

6. ___ Marks the close button.

7. ___ This appears when a window is too small to show all of its contents.

8. ___ These appear next to a menu command when a related dialog box will be displayed when the menu command is clicked.

9. ___ The screen area on which all work is accomplished.

10. ___ The Shut Down command is located here.

A. Shortcut menu

B. X

C. ScreenTip

D. Maximize

E. Desktop

F. Start button

G. Taskbar

H. Start menu

I. Scroll bar

J. Ellipsis (…)

Reinforcement Exercises

Exercise 1

1. Start Windows 98.

2. Move the **Recycle Bin** icon to the right edge of the screen by clicking and dragging it.

3. Open the desktop's shortcut menu by right-clicking an open spot on the desktop.

4. Choose **Arrange Icons** and then **By Type** to return the desktop icons to an orderly arrangement.

Exercise 2

1. Open the **My Computer** window by double-clicking its desktop icon.

2. Close the **My Computer** window by clicking its **Close** button.

3. Open the **My Computer** window by right-clicking its icon and choosing **Open** from the shortcut menu.

4. Close the **My Computer** window by choosing **Close** from its **File** menu.

5. Open the **My Computer** window pressing the (Tab⇆) key until the My Computer icon is high-lighted, and then pressing (↵Enter).

6. Close the **My Computer** window by using the shortcut keys, (Alt)+(F4).

Exercise 3

1. Open the **My Computer** window by double-clicking its icon.

2. Open the **Recycle Bin** window by double-clicking its icon.

3. Move and size the **Recycle Bin** window so that it completely covers the **My Computer** window.

4. Click the **My Computer** button on the taskbar to bring it to the foreground.

5. Click any part of the **Recycle Bin** window to bring it to the foreground.

6. Close both windows.

Exercise 4

1. Open the **Start menu** and choose **Programs**, then **Accessories**. Open the program named **Paint**.

2. Minimize the **Paint** program.

3. Close the **Paint** program by right-clicking its button on the taskbar and choosing **Close** from the shortcut menu.

Exercise 5

1. If necessary, close any open windows.

2. Shut Down Windows 98.

Lesson 2
Working with Menus and the Taskbar

Introduction

In this lesson, you perform tasks that allow you to arrange windows and display information in different ways on your desktop. You will also learn how to work with dialog boxes and menus to format a floppy disk. For this lesson, you will need one blank 3 ¹/₂" disk.

Visual Summary

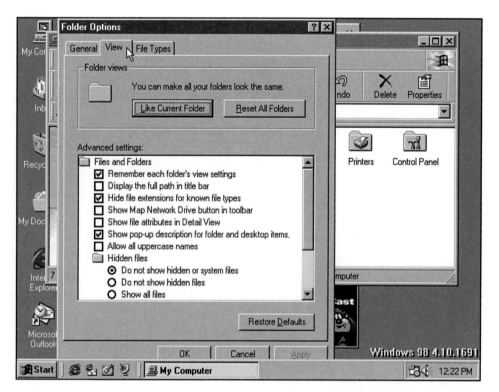

When you are done with Task 5, you will have a Windows 98 desktop that looks like this:

Task 1

Using Menus

Why would I do this?

Although you can perform many tasks by clicking the mouse on different onscreen objects, you will also need to use commands. Commands are organized in menus to make them easy to find. Many windows contain menu bars across the top of the window that list the available menus. Each menu contains related commands to carry out specific functions.

In this task, you learn how to open the My Computer window and familiarize yourself with its menu bar items.

1 Open the **My Computer** window by double-clicking its icon. If necessary, size the window so that it approximates the window shown in the figure.

Quick Tip: When you start this or any subsequent lesson in this book, it's a good idea to close any open windows on the desktop.

2 Notice that there are six menu titles across the top of the window: **File**, **Edit**, **View**, **Go**, **Favorites**, and **Help**. Click the word **View**. The View menu opens.

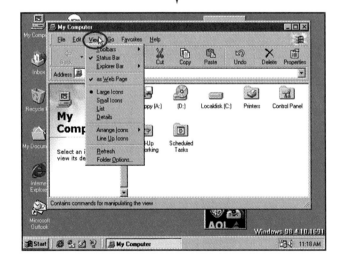

In Depth: A window's Control menu can be opened by clicking the program icon at the upper-left corner of the Window. This menu contains commands.

3 If not already selected, click **Small Icons** to choose the command and close the menu. The icons in the My Computer window change to small icons. To change them to display large icons, click the **View** menu and click **Large Icons.**

In Depth: Menu commands followed by an arrow indicate that a submenu will display when the mouse is placed on these menu commands. When you click a menu command followed by an ellipsis, a dialog box is displayed.

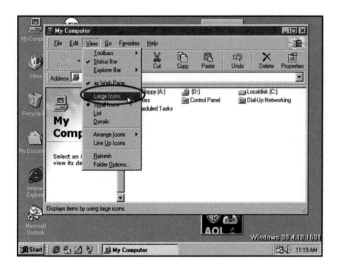

In Depth: If you see a check mark to the left of a menu command, it means that the command is active; for example, in the figure the check mark beside the View, Status Bar command means that the Status bar is showing in the window. More than one command on a menu may have a check mark next to it. Click a command to display the check mark and click it again to remove the check mark.

If you see a dot to the left of a menu option, it indicates that, out of the available options, this one has been selected; for example, in the figure, out of the four available View options, **Small Icons** is selected.

Task 2

Changing the Window Display

Why would I do this?

Changing the way a window displays its contents can make it easier to find what you need. In Windows 98, you can view the contents of a window in a variety of ways. You can also display details, such as file type, size, and the date the item was last modified. You can sort the contents of the window by these details.

In this task, you learn how to change the way a window's contents are displayed.

1 If it is not already open, open the **My Computer** window. If necessary, size it so that it looks similar to the figure. Open your **hard drive (C:)** window by double-clicking the icon, as shown in the figure.

Pothole: Your hard drive icon may have a different name than the one in the figure, but will most likely be assigned the letter C. For the purposes of this book, it will be referred to as the hard drive.

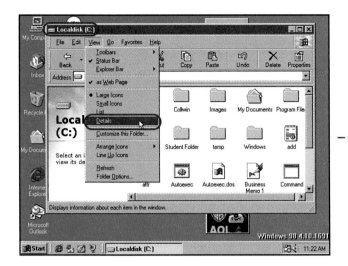

2 The hard drive window is open on your desktop. Open the **View** menu on the hard drive window and place the mouse pointer on the **Details** option.

3 Click the **Details** option. The window now displays the objects in detail form. You may need to resize the window to view all the details.

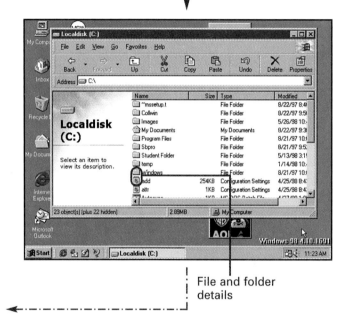

File and folder details

4 Click **View** on the menu bar. Choose **Arrange Icons** and then, from the submenu, select **by Date**.

5 The folders and files in the window are arranged by the date they were last modified, folders before files, most recent listed first. Click **View, Large Icons** from the menu bar to return to the list of files and folders on your hard drive. Close your **hard drive (C:)** window.

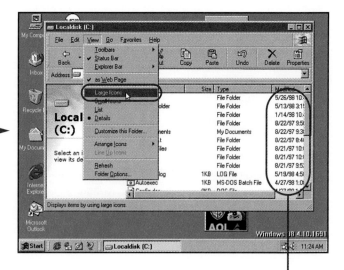

Arranged by date

In Depth: You can arrange the icons in a window any way you want by dragging each one to a new location. Open the **View** menu. Choose **Arrange Icons** and then **Auto Arrange** to deselect the automatic icon setting, if they will not move.

Task 3

Arranging Windows on the Desktop

Why would I do this?

When working with Windows 98, you will often have several open windows on your desktop at one time. The windows may overlap each other and make it difficult to find what you want. You can arrange the windows on the desktop in several ways to make your workspace more organized and efficient.

In this task, you learn how to arrange windows on the desktop.

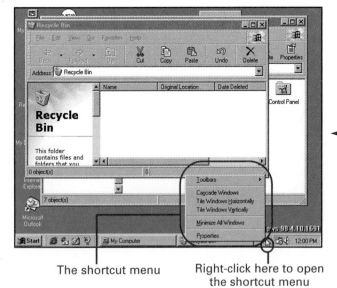

The shortcut menu   Right-click here to open the shortcut menu

1 Make sure the My Computer window is still open. Double-click the **Recycle Bin** icon on the desktop. If you can't see the icon, try moving or sizing. The Recycle Bin window will open up and display on the desktop. Right-click an empty area on the taskbar to reveal the *shortcut* menu.

Pothole: If the Recycle Bin icon is not available on your desktop, use the My Documents icon instead.

In Depth: If you have trouble finding an unoccupied space on the taskbar, you can resize the bar as you would resize a window.

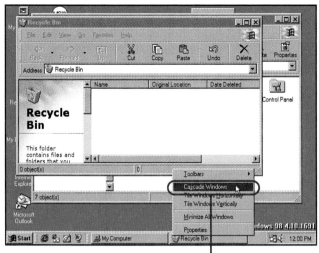

Click Cascade Windows

2 Click **Cascade Windows** to display the windows in an orderly fashion. Windows 98 arranges the open windows to overlap and resizes them so they are all the same size.

3 Click the right mouse button while the mouse is on an unoccupied position on the taskbar and choose **Tile Windows Horizontally**. The windows are displayed horizontally.

Cascading windows

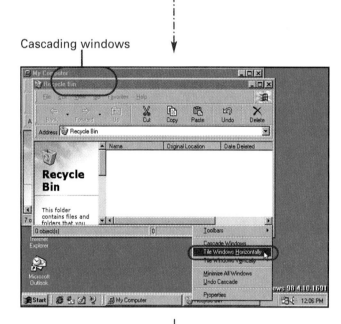

Vertically tiled windows

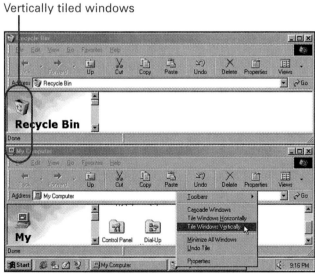

4 Right-click an empty space on the taskbar and choose **Tile Windows Vertically**. The windows are displayed vertically.

5 Click the right mouse button on an unoccupied position on the taskbar and choose **Cascade Windows**. Click the **My Computer** title bar to make it active. An active window moves to the foreground, in front of the others, and its title bar is highlighted.

Horizontally tiled windows

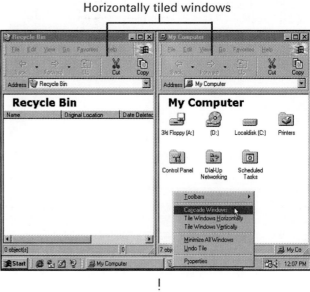

6 Close all open windows by clicking the **Close** button on each, as shown in the figure.

Task 4

Navigating with the Standard Buttons and the Address Bar

Why would I do this?

Many computer users use their PCs to access the Internet with a Web browser such as Internet Explorer. With the Standard Buttons, Windows 98 lets you "browse" through your computer system like you browse through Web pages on the Internet.

In this task, you learn how to use the Standard buttons and the Address bar to move through your computer system.

1 Open the My Computer window. Move and resize the window as shown in the figure. Double-click the **Hard Drive (C:)** icon. A new page is displayed in the window.

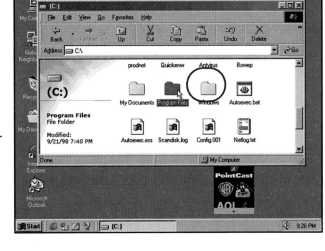

2 Double-click the **Program Files** folder icon. You may need to scroll down to find it.

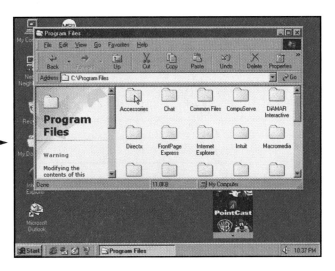

3 The contents of the Program Files folder are displayed in the window. Double-click the **Accessories** folder icon.

4 The contents of the **Accessories** folder are displayed. Read the address bar from right to left. It indicates that you are in the Accessories folder, which is a subfolder of the Program Files folder on drive C.

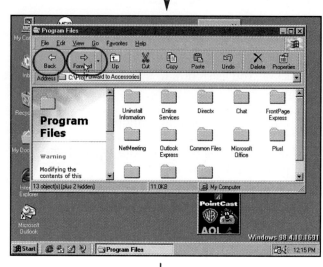

5 On the Button bar, click **Back**. It brings you one step back to the Program Files folder. Click the **Forward** button. It sends you one step forward to the Accessories folder.

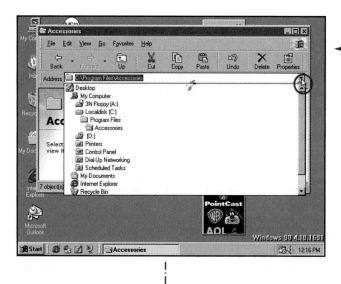

Quick Tip: The Up button works essentially the same as clicking the **Back** button once. It is designed for use with folders, while the Back button can be used for any window content.

6 Click the arrow located on the right side of the Address bar. A list appears showing the folder and icon organization on your PC.

7 Click the **My Computer** icon from the list. You will return to the My Computer window.

In Depth: If you click the arrows next to the Back or Forward buttons, a list of the locations that you can go back (or forward) to are listed. You can then go directly to the location you want by clicking a selection from the list.

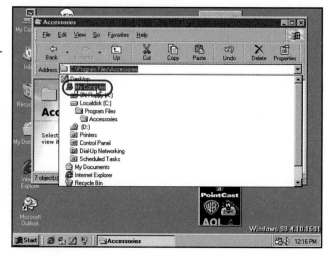

Task 5

Using a Dialog Box

Why would I do this?

Dialog boxes contain options from which you can choose to control windows, applications, document formatting, and a host of other procedures. There are many dialog boxes. Fortunately, all dialog boxes have common elements and all are used in a similar manner.

In this task, you learn how to open and work with a dialog box.

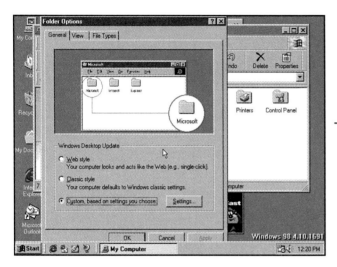

1 If necessary, open the **My Computer** window. Move and resize the window. Select **View**, **Folder Options** from the menu bar. The Folder Options dialog box opens.

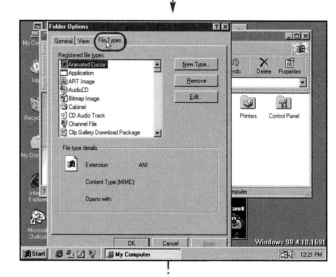

2 The Folder Options dialog box contains three *tabs* (General, View, and File Types) which hold information and options relating to viewing windows, as well as some features common to all dialog boxes. Click the tab labeled **File Types** to view its contents.

Check boxes

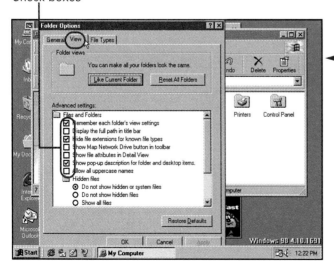

3 Click the **View** tab. Note the check boxes in the Advanced settings area of the dialog box. The contents of the Advanced settings area of the Folder Options dialog box in the figure may differ from what you see on your computers.

In Depth: When a dialog box is open, you cannot select any other window until you respond to the options presented by the dialog box or click the **Cancel** button.

ELEMENT	DESCRIPTION
Check boxes	Square boxes identifying items that can be activated and deactivated. Activate the option by clicking it; a check mark appears in the square box. Deactivate the option by clicking the box; the check mark disappears from the square box.
Command buttons	Command buttons include OK and Cancel. Click **OK** to accept the changes you made in a dialog box. Click **Cancel** to nullify all changes and close the dialog box. Other command buttons may lead you to another dialog box or may perform an action.
List boxes	Lists of available items (such as files) that you can scroll through and select from. Pull-down list boxes are opened by clicking the down arrow at the box's right edge.
Option buttons	Round white buttons that contain a black dot when selected. Option buttons allow you to choose one of several choices. Option buttons are mutually exclusive: choosing one deselects all others.
Tabs	Allows you to choose "pages" within the dialog box that include specific options and information related to the dialog box. To view a page, click the appropriate tab.
Text boxes	Boxes in which you can enter text or values.

Task 6

Formatting a Disk

Why would I do this?

If you use floppy disks to store data, these disks must be formatted to prepare them for use on your PC. Most disks are purchased preformatted. If you have a disk that is not preformatted, or if you want to quickly erase and reuse a disk, you will need to format it.

In this task, you learn how to format a floppy disk.

1 Close the **Folder Options dialog box**. If necessary, open the **My Computer** window. Click the **3 ½ Floppy (A:)** icon on the window.

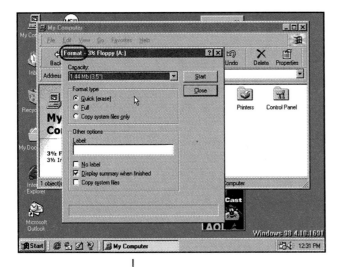

2 Insert a blank disk into drive **A:**. Click the **File** menu and then choose the **Format** command. The **Format** dialog box opens. In addition to option buttons, command buttons, and check boxes, this dialog box has a pull-down list with a caption of *Capacity* and a text box with a caption of *Label*.

> **Pothole:** Do not insert any disk that may have data of value on it. Formatting will erase the data on disk. Also, make sure that the write protect tab in the upper-left corner of the diskette is unlocked.

3 In the Format type area, click the **Full** option button and in the **Label** text box, type your **first name**. When you are done, click the **Start** command button to commence the formatting process.

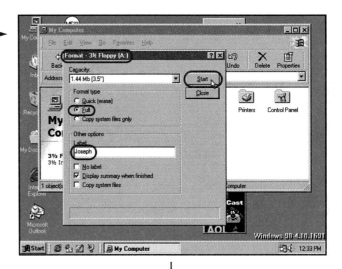

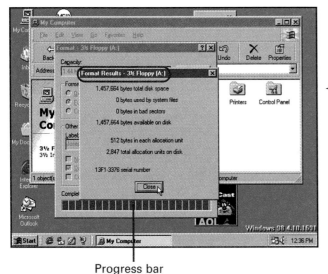

Progress bar

4 A *progress bar* is displayed at the bottom of the **Format** dialog box to indicate the progress of the formatting procedure. When the formatting procedure is done, the progress bar is completely filled, and the **Format Results** dialog box opens. Click the **Close** button on the **Format Results** dialog box to return to the Format dialog box.

5 Click the **Close** button on the Format dialog box to return to the My Computer window. Leave the formatted disk.

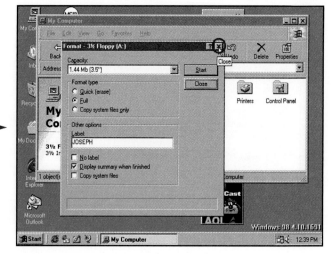

 Quick Tip: When you finish this and every subsequent lesson in this book, make sure to close all the windows on the desktop.

Student Exercises

True-False

For each of the following, check T or F to indicate whether the statement is true or false.

T   F   **1.** All menu commands have associated shortcut buttons on the toolbar.

T   F   **2.** Menu items that lead to dialog boxes are marked by a check mark.

T   F   **3.** Dots and Checkmarks in front of menu items indicate which options are activated.

T   F   **4.** Dialog boxes collect specific command information.

T   F   **5.** A list box is used to type in text or values.

T   F   **6.** Formatting a disk erases all of the data on a disk.

T   F   **7.** Only one window can be active at a time.

T   F   **8.** Pull-down list boxes display their list when you click the arrow button at the boxes' left edge.

T   F   **9.** Tabs allow you to choose Pages within the dialog box.

T   F   **10.** Menus and dialog boxes work differently in all Windows applications.

Identifying Parts of the Windows 98 Screen

Refer to the figure and identify the numbered parts of the screen. Write the letter of the correct label in the space next to the number.

1. _____
2. _____
3. _____
4. _____
5. _____
6. _____
7. _____
8. _____
9. _____
10. _____

A. Command button

B. Active window

C. Desktop

D. Option button

E. Tab

F. Scroll bar

G. Check box

H. Address bar

I. Toolbar

J. List box

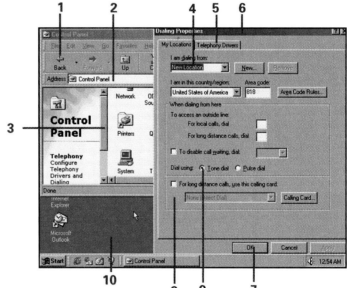

Matching

Match the statements below to the word or phrase that is the best match from the list. Write the letter of the matching word or phrase in the space provided next to the number.

1. ___ The window that is currently being used.

2. ___ The display option that allows the user to view the contents of all windows on the desktop at once.

3. ___ Indicates that a menu item leads to a dialog box.

4. ___ These checkboxes allow you to turn an option on or off.

5. ___ These mutually exclusive buttons allow you to choose one option from a group of available options.

6. ___ This windows object allows you to specify details needed for a command through the use of check boxes, text boxes, list boxes, and command buttons.

7. ___ The process of preparing a disk for use on a PC.

8. ___ This option allows you to see all available information about files and folders.

9. ___ This object contains shortcut buttons to commonly used commands.

10. ___ This display option stacks all windows on the desktop in an orderly fashion.

A. Dialog box

B. Option buttons

C. Formatting

D. Cascade

E. Toolbar

F. Tiled

G. Check boxes

H. An ellipsis (...)

I. Menu bar

J. Details

Reinforcement Exercises

Exercise 1

1. Open the My Computer program.

2. Change the view to show all the files and folders on the hard drive (C:) as large icons.

3. Insert the Learn Windows 98 CD.

4. Double-click the CD drive icon to display the contents of the Learn Windows 98 CD.

5. Change the view to show file and folder details.

6. Arrange the file and folder icons so that they are sorted by size.

Exercise 2

1. Open the My Computer program, the My Documents folder, and the Recycle Bin by double-clicking their icons on the desktop.

2. Arrange the windows so that they are tiled vertically.

3. Use the address bar on the My Documents window to get to the Control Panel.

4. From the My Computer window, view the contents of your hard drive.

5. Arrange the windows so that they are cascaded.

6. Close all windows.

Exercise 3

1. Open the My Computer program. From the **View** menu, choose **Folder Options**.

2. Click the **View** tab to access view settings.

3. Under **Hidden Files**, choose **Show all files** (or another option if this is already selected).

4. Uncheck the option that reads **Hide file extensions for known file types** (or check it if it is already unchecked).

5. Click the **Restore Defaults** control button.

6. Click the **Cancel** button and close all windows on the desktop.

Exercise 4

1. Place a blank floppy disk in the floppy-disk drive.

2. Open the My Computer program. Right-click the floppy-disk drive icon.

3. Choose **Start** or **Close** depending on whether or not you'd like to format your disk.

4. Close all windows and shut down Windows 98.

Lesson 3:
Controlling Programs

Task 1   Starting a Program with the Start Menu

Task 2   Closing a Program

Task 3   Starting a Program Using My Computer

Task 4   Saving Your Work

Task 5   Running DOS Commands

Task 6   Using DOS Applications in Windows

Introduction

One of the best features of Windows 98 is its consistency in starting software applications. Whether you're working in Word, Excel, PowerPoint, Access, or any of the numerous accessories provided with Windows 98, the software applications have a consistent look and are controlled in similar ways. Once you learn how to work with one type of application, the knowledge you gain is transferable to other Windows applications as well.

In this lesson, you learn how to start and close Windows 98 applications, save your work, and work with MS-DOS applications. You will need a blank floppy disk and the Learn Windows 98 CD that accompanies this book for various tasks in the lesson.

Visual Summary

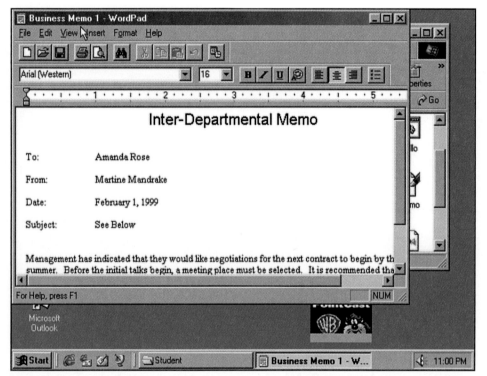

When you are done with Step 5 of Task 4, you will have a Windows 98 desktop that looks like this:

Task 1

Starting a Program with the Start Menu

Why would I do this?

Your programs and documents are logically organized into *folders* on your PC. When a Windows program is installed, a shortcut to the program is placed in the Programs folder on the Start menu. Sometimes the shortcut is stored in a subfolder within the Programs folder; other times not. Either way, clicking the icon runs the program. Whether the software application is a Windows accessory or a word processor, database, spreadsheet, or other program, it's easy to open and use in Windows.

In this task, you learn how to open a program from the Start menu.

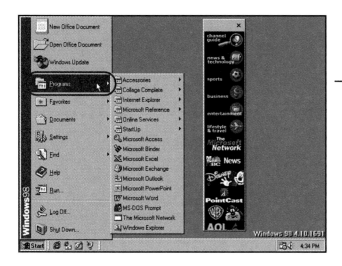

1 Click the **Start** button on the taskbar and point to Programs. The Programs submenu is displayed to the right of the screen.

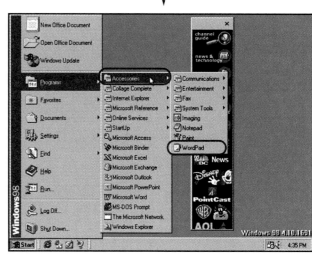

2 Point to Accessories on the submenu to select it. The contents of the Accessories folder opens to the right as a second submenu.

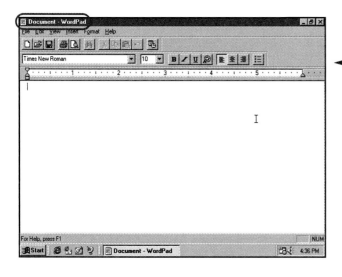

3 Click the **WordPad** program on the submenu. The WordPad application opens. Maximize the window if needed.

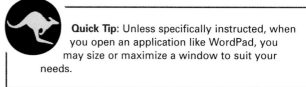

Quick Tip: Unless specifically instructed, when you open an application like WordPad, you may size or maximize a window to suit your needs.

Task 2

Closing a Program

Why would I do this?

You can leave a program open for later use by minimizing it. However, when you finish working with a program, you will want to close that program to free system resources. Too many open applications can tax your system's memory and slow down the computer's processes, such as saving, printing, and switching between applications.

In this task, you close the WordPad application you opened in the previous task.

1 Applications are closed by closing the window. Close the **WordPad** application by clicking the **Close** button.

Quick Tip: You can also close applications by pressing (Alt)+(F4).

Pothole: If you have not saved a file and choose to close the application, a message box appears asking if you want to save it. If you do want to save, choose **Yes**; if not, choose **No**. If you want to return to the document, choose **Cancel**. In this task, if a message box appears, click **No**.

Title bar   Close button

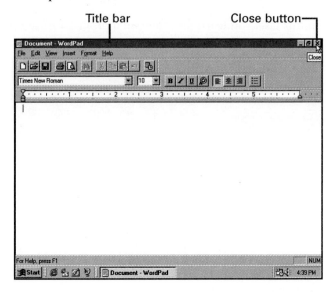

Task 3

Starting a Program Using My Computer

Why would I do this?

As with most Windows tasks, there are several ways in which you can start applications. If you would like to edit an existing document, you can quickly open the necessary application and the document by double-clicking the document file's icon. Document file icons can be accessed using My Computer or Windows Explorer. In Lesson 9, you will learn how to place shortcuts to documents on the Windows 98 desktop. The skills you learn in this task, combined with Lesson 9 skills, will allow you to access your data more quickly.

In this task, you learn how to launch an application by using My Computer. You will need the Learn Windows 98 CD that accompanies this book.

1 Insert the Learn Windows 98 CD into your CD-ROM drive. Double-click the **My Computer** icon to open the My Computer window.

Pothole: Just as with the Hard Drive, your CD-ROM drive may be labeled with almost any letter (typically D or E). No matter what the letter, the CD-ROM drive is easy to identify by the picture of a CD on its icon. For the purposes of this book, we will refer to it simply as the CD-ROM drive.

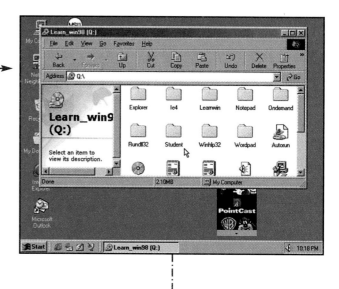

2 Double-click the **CD-ROM drive** icon. The Learn_win98 CD window opens.

3 Double-click the **Student** folder. The Student folder contains all the files that you will work with in this book.

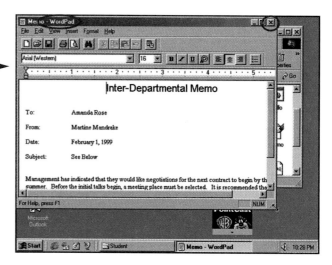

4 Double-click the **Memo** file icon. Since it was saved in WordPad format, WordPad automatically launches and opens the Memo document. You are now ready to edit it.

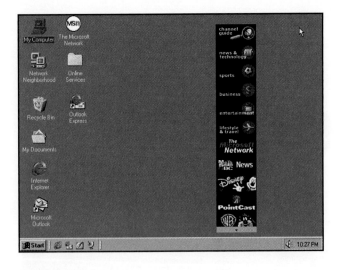

5 Close the document by clicking the **Close** button on the WordPad title bar. Close all other windows.

> **Quick Tip:** The quickest way to start an application is to place a shortcut icon to the application on your desktop. There is a shortcut icon to the Outlook Express application on the desktop in the figure. You'll learn how to create shortcuts in Lesson 9.

Task 4

Saving Your Work

Why would I do this?

You save documents as files so that you can refer to them later for printing, modifying, and copying. All Windows applications save documents in much the same way.

In this task, you learn how to save a WordPad document on your blank floppy disk.

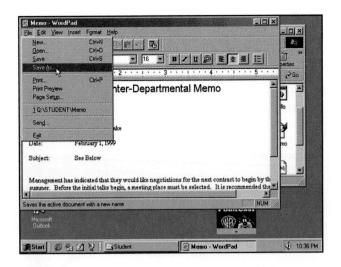

1 Place a blank floppy disk in your floppy-disk drive. Make sure that the Learn Windows 98 CD is still in your CD-ROM drive. Open the **Memo** file as you did in the last task. Click Wordpad's **File** menu to open it.

> **Quick Tip:** Some menu commands can be issued from the keyboard. The keystrokes used for these commands are indicated next to the associated command in the menu. For instance, the File menu in the figure shows that the Ctrl and P keys pressed simultaneously will issue the Print command.

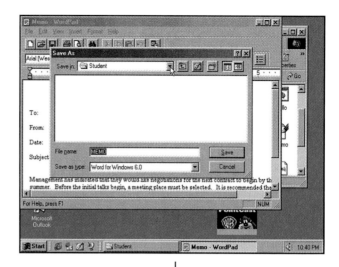

Quick Tip: The Save As command is used when you wish to specify the location or file-name to which to save. Use the Save command when you wish to save the document to the same location and filename from which it was opened. You cannot save files to a CD-ROM (Read-Only Memory).

2 Click **Save As** in the File menu. The Save As dialog box opens.

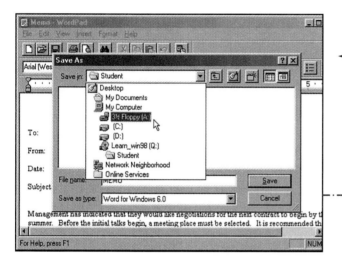

3 Click the arrow to the right of the **Save in:** list box to open it and choose **3 ¹⁄₂" Floppy (A:)**.

4 Double-click the name **MEMO** in the **File name** text box to select it. Type **Business Memo 1.wri** to overwrite **MEMO**.

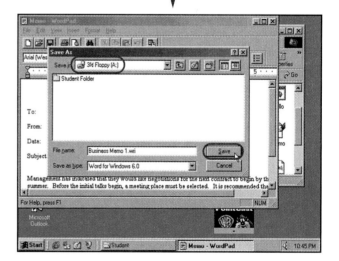

In Depth: Normally, if you were working at home or at work and had your own personal computer, you would store your personal documents on drive C, in a folder called My Documents. However, for classroom purposes where computers are often shared among many students, all of your own personal files will be stored on and retrieved from your floppy disk, typically drive A.

5 Click the **Save** button. The file is saved to your floppy disk and the dialog box closes.

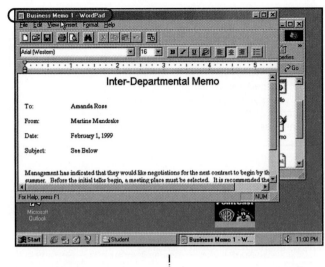

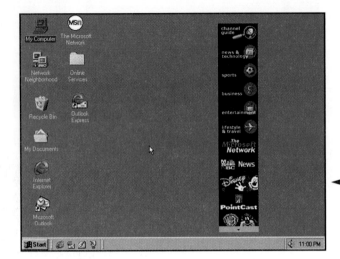

6 Close both the WordPad application window and the My Computer window.

Task 5

Running DOS Commands

Why would I do this?

MS-DOS (Microsoft Disk Operating System) is the command-driven operating system that preceded the Windows operating systems. There may be times when you want to access the DOS prompt from Windows. For example, you may want to run a non-Windows (DOS) program. Windows provides a DOS prompt window that you can open while working in Windows.

In this task, you learn how get into the DOS environment from Windows, run DOS commands, and then exit back to Windows 98.

1 Open the **Start** menu. Move the mouse pointer to **Programs**, and the submenu will appear.

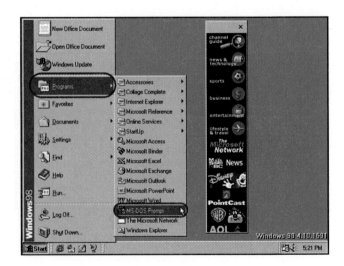

2 Click the **MS-DOS Prompt** icon in the Programs menu. The DOS window appears with a blinking cursor at the DOS Command prompt.

Quick Tip: You can use the toolbar icons at the top of the DOS window to mark, copy, paste, enlarge to full screen, set the background, and set the font of the DOS window.

3 Type **cd** and press ⏎Enter to change to the root directory. You can run any program by typing the appropriate DOS command.

Pothole: Your mouse will only work in the DOS prompt if a mouse driver has been loaded. You can refer to your instructor or lab person if you need assistance with loading the mouse driver.

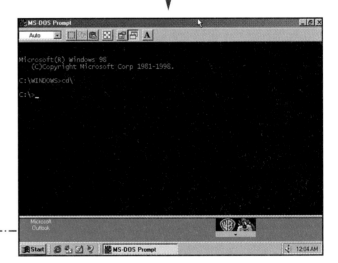

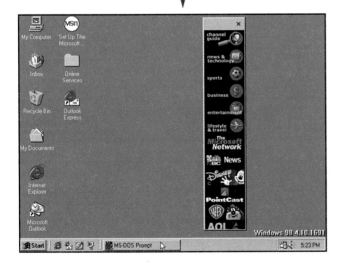

4 When you are ready to work with Windows again, click the **Minimize** button on the DOS window. The window reduces to a button on the taskbar, and you can work in other windows until you need the DOS window again. Click the **MS-DOS Prompt** button on the taskbar to open the DOS window.

5 Type **exit** at the DOS prompt and press ⏎Enter to close the MS-DOS prompt window.

Quick Tip: Press Alt+⏎Enter to enlarge the DOS window to full screen; when you finish, press Alt+⏎Enter again to restore the DOS window to its original size.

Task 6

Using DOS Applications in Windows

Why would I do this?

There will be times when you want to access the DOS prompt from Windows to use DOS commands. A typical DOS command is MEM, which displays certain information about the internal memory on your PC.

In this task, you learn how to open the MS-DOS prompt and work with the MEM program.

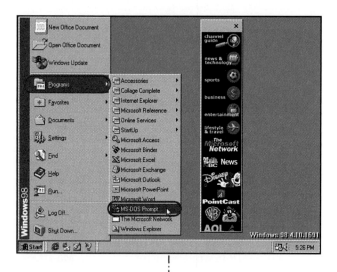

1 Open the Start menu, choose **Programs**, **MS-DOS Prompt**. The DOS window is displayed.

In Depth: Some DOS applications require that you be in a specific directory before you can run the application. For instance, if you wanted to run WordPerfect 6.0 for DOS, you would first type in **cd\wp60** and then press ⏎Enter before typing wp to start the WordPerfect program.

2 To run a DOS program called **MEM**, type **mem** (upper or lower case, it doesn't matter) and then press ⏎Enter at the DOS prompt. A program displays statistics regarding the memory configuration of your computer.

3 Type **exit**, and press (↵Enter) at the MS-DOS prompt to return to the Windows 98 environment.

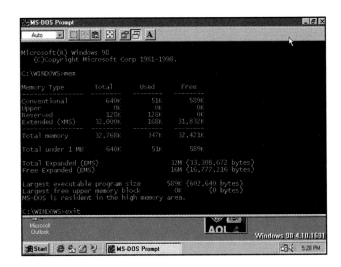

Student Exercises

True-False

For each of the following, circle either T or F to indicate whether the statement is true or false.

T   F   **1.** The only way to start a program is from the Start menu.

T   F   **2.** There is more than one method for closing a program.

T   F   **3.** The hard drive is usually referred to as the C: drive.

T   F   **4.** Most users save their work to the CD-ROM drive.

T   F   **5.** The quickest way to start an application is to place a shortcut icon to the application on your desktop.

T   F   **6.** An application can be opened by double-clicking an icon of a document file that was created with it.

T   F   **7.** MS-DOS is a windows application.

T   F   **8.** On a home PC, you normally save your documents in a folder called My Computer.

T   F   **9.** MS-DOS commands can only be typed in upper-case letters.

T   F   **10.** Files must be saved if you plan to access them again after you've closed the application.

Identifying Parts of the Windows 98 Screen

Refer to the figure and identify the numbered parts of the screen. Write the letter of the correct label in the space next to the number.

1. _____
2. _____
3. _____
4. _____
5. _____
6. _____
7. _____
8. _____
9. _____
10. _____

A. MS-DOS window

B. Folder

C. Shortcut

D. Command prompt

E. Close button

F. Hard drive

G. Floppy drive

H. CD-ROM drive

I. Open button

J. Save button

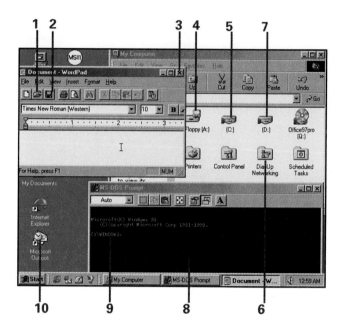

Matching

Match the statements below to the word or phrase that is the best match from the list. Write the letter of the matching word or phrase in the space provided next to the number.

1. ___ You can read files from this device, but you can't save files to it.

2. ___ You exit a program by clicking this object.

3. ___ Most users store their files in this folder.

4. ___ Type these at the MS-DOS prompt.

5. ___ Choose this command when you wish to store your work on disk with its current name.

6. ___ This Operating System preceded Windows.

7. ___ Choose this command when you wish to store your work on disk with a new name.

8. ___ This object is used to organize files.

9. ___ These are special icons that allow you to start a program quickly.

10. ___ Most files and applications on your computer are stored on this device.

A. Folder

B. CD-ROM

C. Hard Drive

D. Save

E. Close button

F. My Documents

G. Save As

H. Shortcut Icons

I. MS-DOS

J. Commands

Reinforcement Exercises

Exercise 1

1. Place your floppy disk in the floppy-disk drive.

2. Start the Wordpad application by choosing **Start/Programs/Accessories/Wordpad**.

3. Type your name in the file.

4. Save the file to your floppy disk as **exercise1**.

5. Close the WordPad application.

Exercise 2

1. Place your Learn Windows 98 CD in the CD-ROM drive.

2. Use My Computer to view the contents of the Student folder on the CD.

3. Double-click the **BigBen** file icon to open it.

4. Close the Paint application.

Exercise 3

1. Go to the MS-DOS prompt.

2. Use the **dir** command to view the contents of the Windows folder.

3. Return to Windows.

Lesson 4
Working with Folders and Files

Introduction

Windows 98 logically organizes programs, data, and other files into *folders*. Folders are organizational tools that help you keep track of your files. For instance, a folder named My Documents can be used to store files that you create. Another folder named Program Files contains most of the files used in the programs on your computer. Folders can also contain other folders. You could create a folder within the My Documents folder named Computer Class to store all of the files that you create in this class. Because Windows organizes its file storage around folders, it is important to learn to work with folders and files.

In the previous Lesson you learned how to access files within a folder when you opened a file in the Student folder on the Learn Windows 98 CD. In this lesson, you learn how to create, copy, move, rename, locate, manage and delete files and folders using the My Computer window. You also learn how to switch between open documents. Lastly, you are introduced to the Windows Explorer program as an alternate to the My Computer program.

Visual Summary

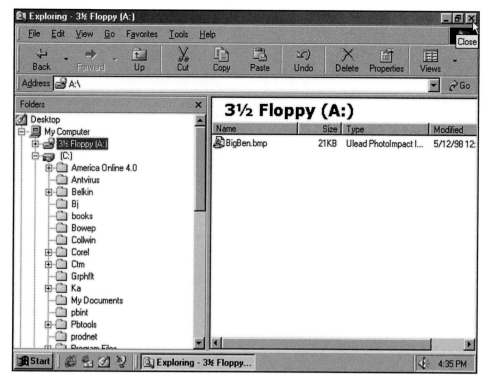

When you are done with Step 8 of Task 7, you will have a Windows 98 desktop that looks like this:

Task 1

Creating Folders

Why would I do this?

Finding files is easier if you group related files into folders. For example, you may want to create a folder to hold all of your word processing documents. Creating a folder enables you to keep your own documents separate from the program files so that you can easily find them to do your work.

In this task, you learn how to create a folder on your floppy disk.

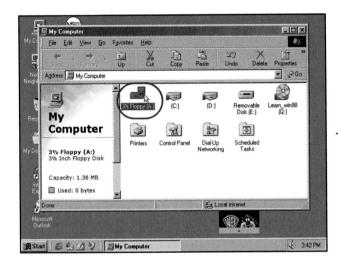

1 Place a floppy disk in the floppy disk drive, open **My Computer** and then the **3 ½" Floppy (A:)** drive by double-clicking its icon.

2 Click **File** on the menu bar and then **New** on the File menu. A submenu opens.

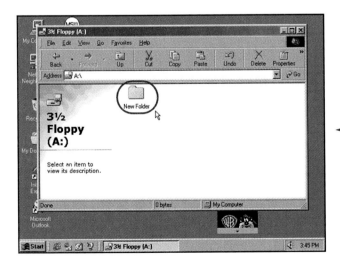

3 From the submenu, choose **Folder**. The new folder is displayed in the floppy drive window with the name **New Folder**.

Pothole: The folder icons can appear as small icons or as large icons. To change how they are displayed, click **Large Icons** or **Small Icons** in the **View** menu.

4 Right-click the **New Folder** icon. A shortcut menu is displayed.

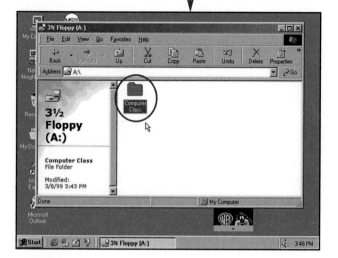

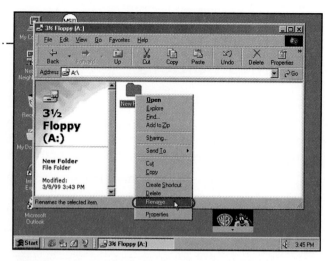

5 From the shortcut menu, click **Rename** and then enter the name **Computer Class**; when you type, the old name is removed. Press ↵Enter when you are finished typing to accept the new name. Leave the floppy disk in the drive for use in the next Task. Close all windows on the desktop.

Quick Tip: You can rename a folder at any time, not just when you create it. Simply right-click the folder to be renamed, pick **Rename** from the shortcut menu, and type in the new folder name.

In Depth: A folder or file can have a name containing up to 255 characters, including spaces. You can also name a folder or file with letters, numbers, or other symbols on your keyboard with the exception of \ ? : * " < > or |.

Task 2

Saving Files to a Folder

Why would I do this?

You can place a file in a folder either by copying or moving an existing file from some other location (as discussed later in this Lesson), or by saving it to the folder from the application that is used to create it.

In this task, you learn how to save a file to the Computer Class folder on your floppy disk.

1 Make sure that the floppy disk you used in the last Task is in the floppy disk drive. Open the WordPad program by choosing **Start**, **Programs**, **Accessories**, and **WordPad**.

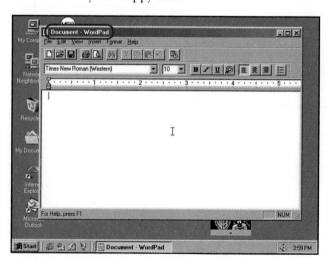

2 Type your name in the WordPad document window.

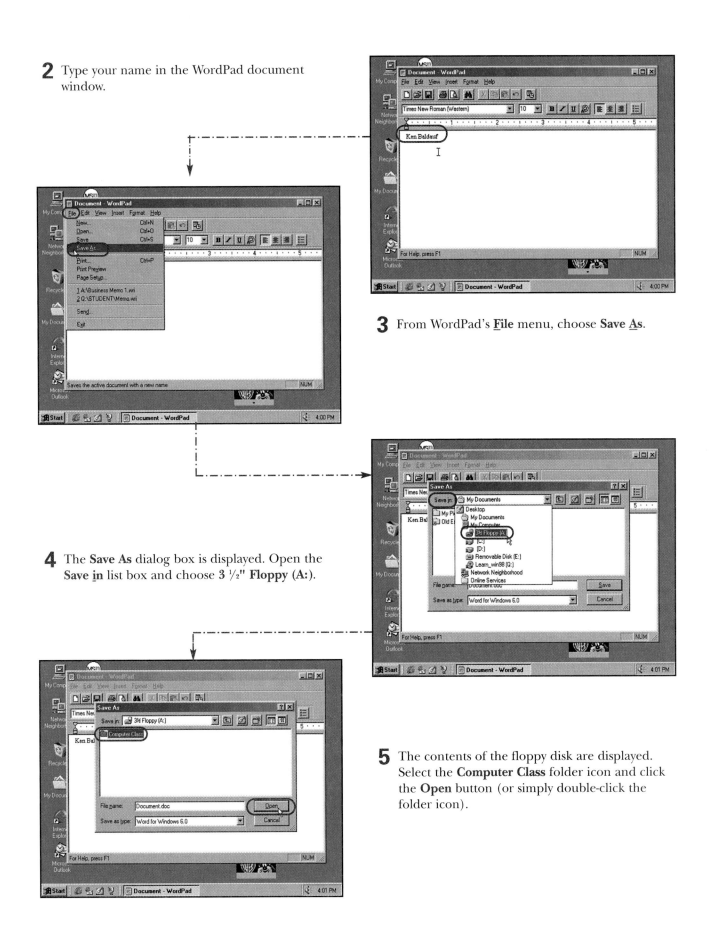

3 From WordPad's **File** menu, choose **Save As**.

4 The **Save As** dialog box is displayed. Open the **Save in** list box and choose **3 ½" Floppy (A:)**.

5 The contents of the floppy disk are displayed. Select the **Computer Class** folder icon and click the **Open** button (or simply double-click the folder icon).

6 The **Save in** list box now lists **Computer Class** as the location to save to. Since the folder is empty, no file or folder icons are displayed.

Quick Tip: By clicking the **Up One Level** button (the button with the folder and arrow icon), you can move up one level back to the A: drive.

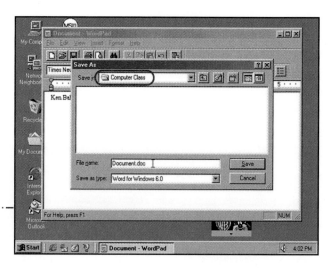

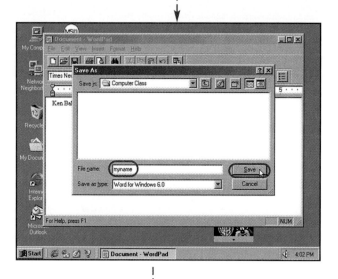

7 Click the **File name** text box and replace its contents with **myname**. Click the **Save** button.

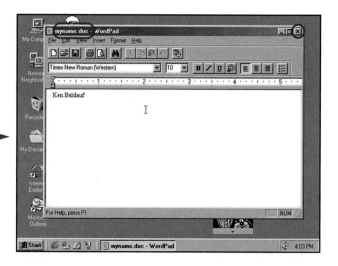

8 The file is saved in the Computer Class folder on the floppy disk. Close **WordPad**.

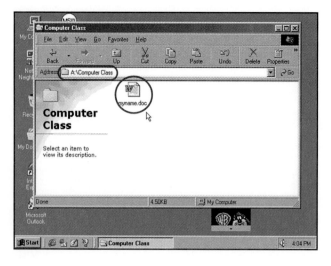

9 Open **My Computer**, then the **3 ½" Floppy (A:)** drive. Double-click the **Computer Class** folder to open it. Notice the **myname** file icon. Also, notice the Address box tells the exact location of the file. Close all windows on the desktop. Leave the floppy disk in the drive for the next Task.

Task 3

Copying Files

Why would I do this?

There are a number of reasons why you might want to copy a file or a folder. First and most importantly, it's a good idea to have duplicates of all of your files as backups in case of disk failure (an unfortunate but fairly common experience). Other reasons for copying a file are to share it with another user or to access it yourself on another computer.

In this task, you learn how to copy a file from your Learn Windows 98 CD to your floppy disk.

1 Make sure that the floppy disk used in the last Task is in the floppy disk drive and the Learn Windows 98 CD is in the CD-ROM drive. Open **My Computer** and then the CD-ROM drive by double-clicking its icon.

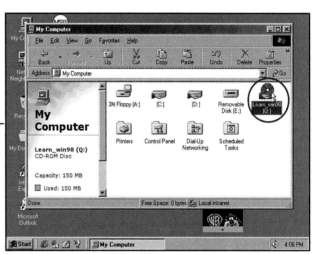

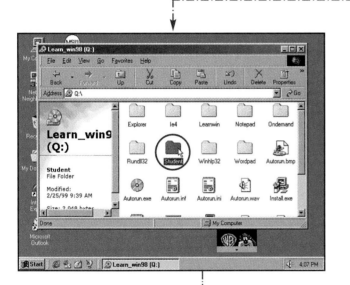

2 Double-click the **Student** folder in the CD-ROM drive window to open it.

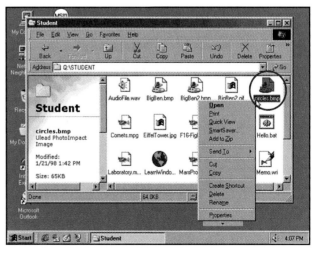

3 Right-click the **circles** file icon to display its shortcut menu.

4 Choose **Copy** from the shortcut menu. A copy of the file is placed in an area of computer memory called the *Clipboard*.

In Depth: *Copy* leaves the file that is copied intact. *Cut* removes the file from its original location.

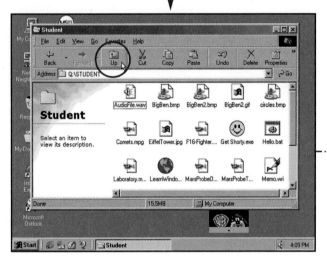

5 Click the **Up One Level** button twice to view the My Computer window.

6 Right-click the **3 ½" Floppy (A:)** drive icon to open its shortcut menu.

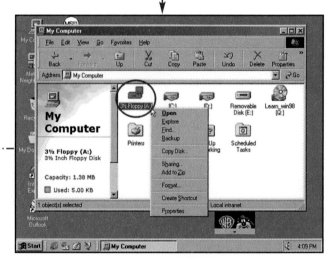

7 Choose **Paste** from the shortcut menu. A copy of the file is copied from the Clipboard onto the A: drive.

In Depth: Cut, Copy, and Paste commands are available in the Edit menu, as buttons on the toolbar, and in file and folder shortcut menus.

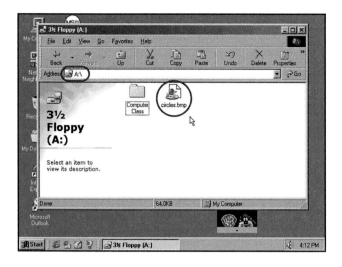

8 Double-click the **A: drive** icon to view its contents. Note that a copy of the circles files is now on your floppy disk. Leave the desktop as it is for the next Task.

> **In Depth:** Keyboard shortcuts are handy for copying or moving files and data. Ctrl+X cuts the highlighted object, Ctrl+C copies it, Ctrl+V pastes it. Note that X, C, and V are neighboring keys near the control key and are easy to remember.

Task 4

Moving Files

Why would I do this?

Over the course of your computer-using life, you will organize and reorganize the files and folders on your computer many times. Such organizational efforts usually involve creating new folders, moving files into them, and perhaps deleting old, unneeded folders and files. Knowing how to move files is important not only for organizational reasons but also for instances when you need to transfer a file from one computer to another.

In this task, you learn how to move a file from the floppy drive to a folder on the floppy drive.

1 The floppy disk from the last task should be in the floppy drive and the contents of the floppy disk drive should be displayed in a window on your screen. Click and drag the **circles** icon from its current location to the **Computer Class** folder icon.

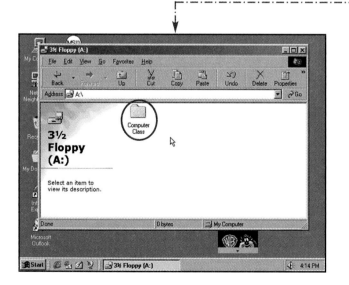

2 Confirm the File Move by clicking the **Yes** button. The circles file is moved to the Computer Class folder and its icon is no longer displayed in the floppy drive window. Double-click the **Computer Class** folder to verify that the file was moved.

3 The circles file is displayed in the Computer Class folder. Close all windows on the desktop.

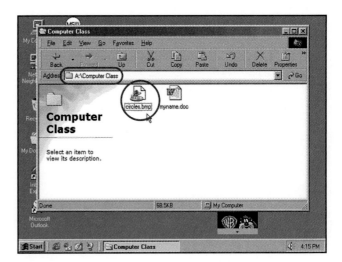

In Depth: Folders can be copied or moved using the same methods as we've learned for files. In the case of folders, all of a folder's contents are moved and copied along with the folder.

In Depth: Use this table to sort out the rather confusing methods of copying and moving files and folders by dragging them with the mouse:

MOUSE AND KEY ACTION	SOURCE & DESTINATION	RESULT
Drag icon with no key depressed	Different drives	Copies
Drag icon with **⬆Shift** depressed	Different drives	Moves
Drag icon with no key depressed	Same drive	Moves
Drag icon with **Ctrl** depressed	Same drive	Copies

Task 5

Finding Files and Folders

Why would I do this?

After working for an extended period of time with your applications, your computer becomes filled with various folders and files, making it nearly impossible for you to know where everything is located. Windows includes a command that helps you locate specific files by name, file type, and location of the file.

In this task, you learn how to find files and folders.

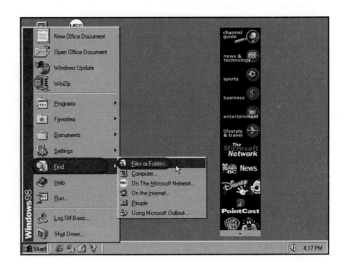

1 Open the Start menu and select **Find**, then **Files or Folders**. The Find: All Files dialog box opens.

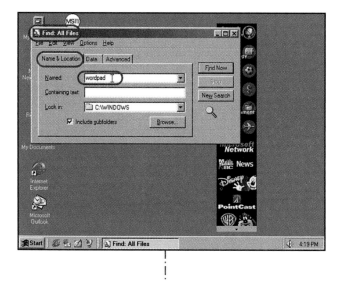

2 If necessary, click the **Name & Location** tab. Type **wordpad** in the **Named** text box.

> **Quick Tip:** You can use the characters *
> and ? (known as wildcards) to find files.
> For example, to find all files ending with the
> extension doc, you type ***.doc** in the Named text
> box. To find all files beginning with doc followed by any
> two characters, and ending in any extension, you type
> **doc??.***.

3 Click the down arrow next to the **Look in** text box. Select the **C:** drive as the location where you want to search for the wordpad file.

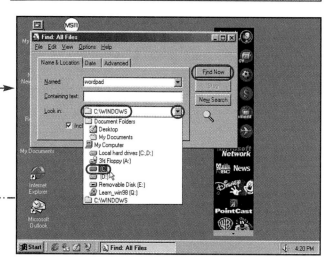

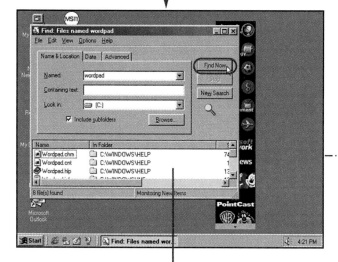

Files found on drive C containing a reference to wordpad

4 Click the **Find Now** button to initiate the search for wordpad. Windows searches the hard drive (C:) and displays a list of the found wordpad files at the bottom of the dialog box. Notice that the title of the dialog box reflects the search.

5 Click the **New Search** button to search for a new file or folder.

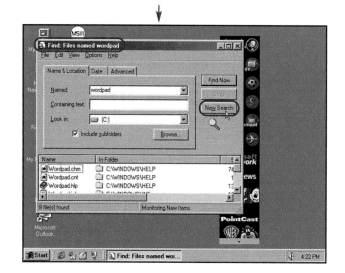

6 A warning message appears stating that the previous search will be cleared. Click **OK**. The Find: All Files dialog box reopens, ready for the next search. Click the **Close** button on the Find: All Files dialog box to return to the desktop.

> **Pothole:** If you don't know the name of the file for which you are searching but you know the type of file, choose the **Advanced** tab in the Find: All Files dialog box. From the Of type list box, choose the type of file, such as Application, Configuration, Help, MS Word Document, or Text Document. Click the **Find Now** button and Windows performs the search.

Task 6

Deleting Folders and Files

Why would I do this?

You delete folders and files when you no longer need them or when you have copied them elsewhere as a backup and do not need two copies. Remember, when you delete a folder you also delete its contents.

In this task, you learn how to delete a folder you created in earlier tasks from your floppy disk.

1 Open the **3 ½" Floppy (A:)** drive window using **My Computer** and select, but do not open, the Computer Class Folder.

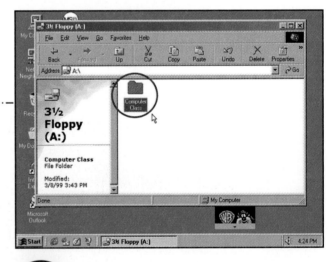

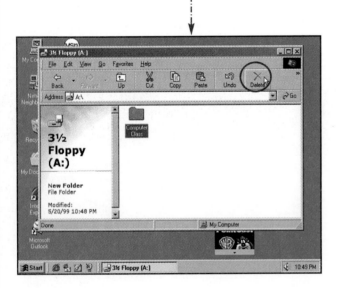

> **In Depth:** You can select multiple file or folder icons by holding down Ctrl and clicking each icon that you want to select. You can select a row of folder or file icons by selecting the first icon in the list and then, while holding down Shift, selecting the last icon.

2 Select **Delete** from the menu bar or press the Del key.

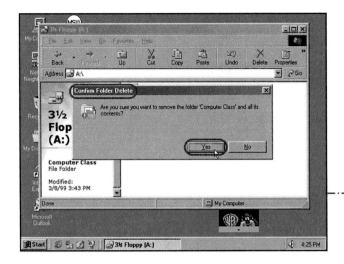

3 The Confirm Folder Delete confirmation box is displayed. Click **Yes** to delete the selected folder.

QuickTip: Once a file or folder is deleted from a floppy disk, there's no getting it back. When you delete an item from your hard drive, you can get it back by opening the Recycle Bin icon on the desktop, highlighting the deleted file icon and choosing **File**, **Restore**.

4 The confirmation box closes and the Computer Class folder and its contents are deleted from the floppy drive. Close all open windows on your desktop.

Task 7

Using Windows Explorer

Why would I do this?

You can use the Windows Explorer program in much the same way that you use the My Computer program: to copy and move files and folders, to create and rename folders, and to open and view files and folders. The difference between these two programs is that My Computer allows you to view only the contents of one location in a window, while Windows Explorer allows you to see the contents of a location and your entire system. Most users find Windows Explorer a more convenient program for use in file management tasks such as copying and moving files and folders.

In this task, you learn how to use Windows Explorer to view and copy files on your computer.

1 If necessary, place a floppy disk in the floppy disk drive and the **Learn Windows 98** CD in the CD-ROM drive. Click the **Start** button. Choose **Programs**, **Windows Explorer** from the menus.

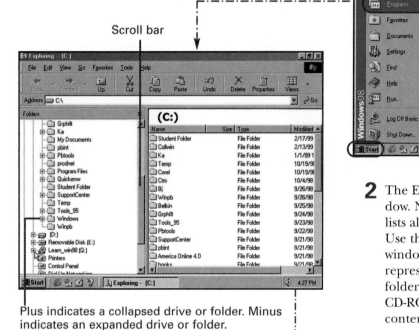

Scroll bar

Plus indicates a collapsed drive or folder. Minus indicates an expanded drive or folder.

2 The Exploring window opens. Maximize the window. Notice that the left side of the split window lists all the drives and folders on your computer. Use the scrollbar to scroll down this side of the window. Any folder with a plus sign in front of it represents a collapsed folder containing more folders and files. Click the plus sign next to the CD-ROM drive icon to expand it and see its contents.

3 Select the **Student** folder icon listed under the CD-ROM drive icon (you may have to scroll down to see it) to display all of the folders and files contained within the Student folder. The contents of the Student folder are displayed in the right sub-window.

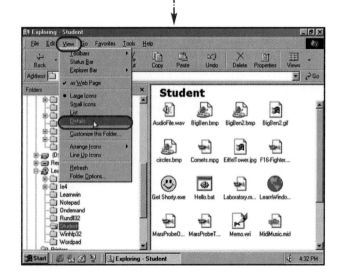

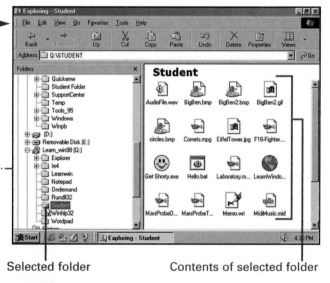

Selected folder　　　　Contents of selected folder

In Depth: You can start applications from Windows Explorer just as you did with My Computer in Lesson 3, Task 3, by double-clicking a document or program icon.

4 If the Details view is not already selected, select **View**, **Details** to display the details of each file in the right window. Details view may already be selected.

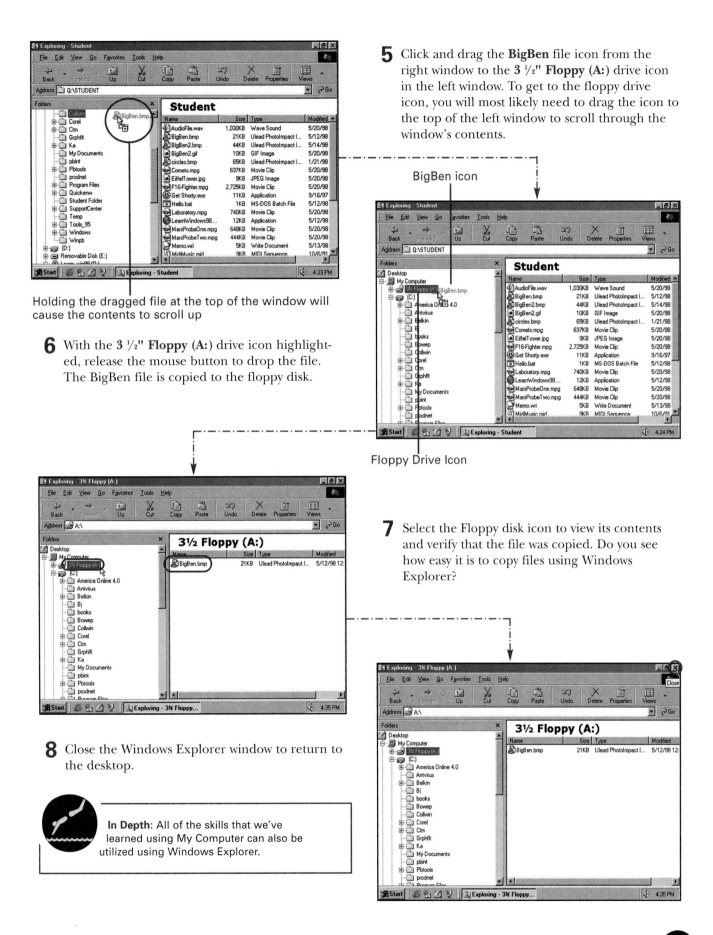

5 Click and drag the **BigBen** file icon from the right window to the **3 ½" Floppy (A:)** drive icon in the left window. To get to the floppy drive icon, you will most likely need to drag the icon to the top of the left window to scroll through the window's contents.

BigBen icon

Holding the dragged file at the top of the window will cause the contents to scroll up

6 With the **3 ½" Floppy (A:)** drive icon highlighted, release the mouse button to drop the file. The BigBen file is copied to the floppy disk.

Floppy Drive Icon

7 Select the Floppy disk icon to view its contents and verify that the file was copied. Do you see how easy it is to copy files using Windows Explorer?

8 Close the Windows Explorer window to return to the desktop.

In Depth: All of the skills that we've learned using My Computer can also be utilized using Windows Explorer.

Student Exercises

True-False

For each of the following, check T or F to indicate whether the statement is true or false.

T   F   **1.** Folders aid in the organization of files on disk.

T   F   **2.** **my new file!.doc** is a valid name for a file.

T   F   **3.** My Computer or Windows Explorer can be used to rename a file or folder.

T   F   **4.** Disk drives rarely ever fail or crash.

T   F   **5.** The **Copy** command is the best protection against disk failure.

T   F   **6.** The **Paste** command is always used prior to the **Copy** command.

T   F   **7.** To select more than one folder or file at a time, hold down (Alt) as you select the files.

T   F   **8.** The **Copy** or **Cut** command is always used prior to the **Paste** command.

T   F   **9.** Most users prefer using My Computer over Windows Explorer for file management tasks.

T   F   **10.** The quickest way to move a file is to drag its icon from one location to another.

Identifying Parts of the Windows Screen

Refer to the figure and identify the numbered parts of the screen. Write the letter of the correct label in the space next to the number.

1. _____
2. _____
3. _____
4. _____
5. _____
6. _____
7. _____
8. _____
9. _____
10. _____

A. Drive

B. A closed folder

C. Current location

D. An open folder

E. Windows Explorer window

F. Toolbar

G. Selected folder

H. Contents of selected folder

I. Move up one folder level

J. Size of selected object

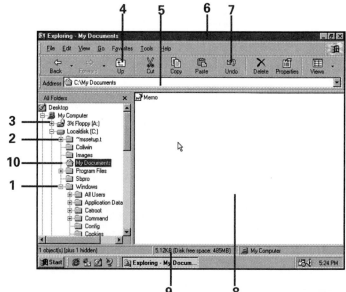

Matching

Match the statements below to the word or phrase that is the best match from the list. Write the letter of the matching word or phrase in the space provided next to the number.

1. ___ These help to organize files on disk.

2. ___ These may be used to find multiple files with similar names.

3. ___ A popular program for file management.

4. ___ If you click and drag a file from the floppy drive to the hard drive, it will have this effect on the file.

5. ___ The quickest way to move a file.

6. ___ This symbol appearing next to a folder in Windows Explorer means that the folder is collapsed and contains more files or folders.

7. ___ The quickest way to get rid of a file or folder.

8. ___ A temporary holding place for data that has been cut or copied.

9. ___ This command copies whatever is on the clipboard to the insertion point.

10. ___ This command deletes a file from its current location and places a copy of its contents on the clipboard.

A. Del

B. Drag

C. Paste

D. wildcards

E. +

F. Cut

G. Clipboard

H. Folder

I. Windows Explorer

J. Copy

Reinforcement Exercises

Exercise 1

1. Use My Computer to create a new folder named **Sample Programs** on your floppy disk.

2. Using My Computer, from the **Student** folder on the **Learn Windows 98** CD-ROM, copy the two files, **Get Shorty** and **LearnWindows98** into the newly created **Sample Programs** folder.

3. Within the **Sample Programs** folder, create a new folder named **Icons**.

Exercise 2

1. Use Windows Explorer to view the contents of the floppy disk.

2. View the contents of the **Sample Programs** folder.

3. View the file details and arrange them by name.

4. Using Windows Explorer, from the **Student** folder on the **Learn Windows 98** CD-ROM, copy the **BigBen** file into the **Icons** folder on the floppy disk.

5. Delete all folders and files on the floppy disk.

Lesson 5
Getting Help

Introduction

Windows provides various Help features to assist you in performing both complex and everyday tasks, such as using icons, managing hardware and software, troubleshooting hardware and software problems, locating files, and moving files. In fact, Windows *Online Help* is so useful that many users never have to refer to the Windows documentation or printed help references at all. In addition to the Help topics provided through the Help window, there is another online method of getting assistance that can be used called *context-sensitive help*.

In this lesson, you learn how to access the Help window and make inquiries using the Contents, Index, and Search features. You also learn how to print a help topic. Lastly, you are introduced to the Windows context-sensitive help feature called "What's This?".

Visual Summary

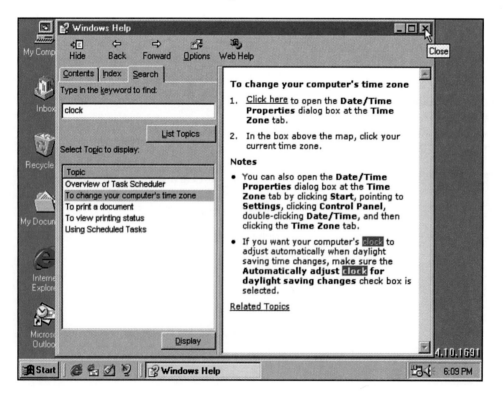

When you are done with Task 4, you will have a Windows 98 desktop that looks like this:

Task 1

Starting Help and Using the Contents Feature

Why would I do this?

Whether you are a new or experienced Windows user, you will need help at some point with a procedure or task; for example, setting up a printer, finding a document, or linking between applications. Windows 98 makes it easy and convenient to find that help. When you use the *Contents Help* feature to find Windows help, you are presented with a series of general topics that you can narrow down to find more specific help on the topic or topics that you need.

In this task, you learn how to open the Help Topics dialog box and work with Windows Contents help.

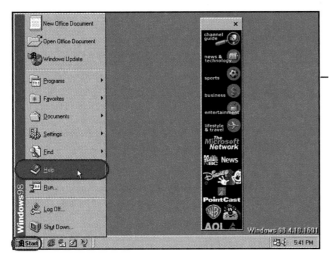

1 Click the **Start** button on the taskbar and then click **Help** on the Start menu.

2 The Windows Help window opens. Notice that it includes three tabs (Contents, Index, and Search) from which you can choose to get assistance. If it is not already selected, click the **Contents** tab.

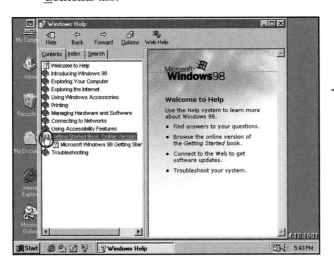

3 Click the book icon to the left of **Getting Started Book: Online Version**. The subtopic available under this heading appears.

Quick Tip: The last tab you viewed in the Help window is the one that opens the next time you open the Help window.

Quick Tip: When the Windows Help window appears in two panes, you can size each of the panes. Put the mouse pointer between the two panes and, when the mouse pointer appears as a double-headed arrow, drag the mouse to the right or left to size each pane.

4 Click the **Microsoft Windows 98 Getting Started Book** subtopic. A description of the topic contents is presented in the right-side pane.

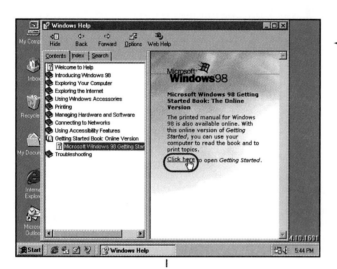

5 In the right-side pane, click **Click here** to jump to the next help window. The Getting Started window appears.

6 Click the **Glossary** topic in the left-side pane. The words in the glossary appear.

In Depth: Text or pictures that you click on to jump from one location to another are called links or hyperlinks. The mouse pointer usually changes to a pointing hand when positioned over a link. Text that acts as a link is referred to as hypertext.

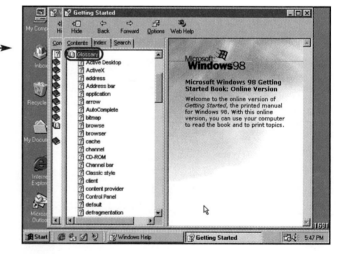

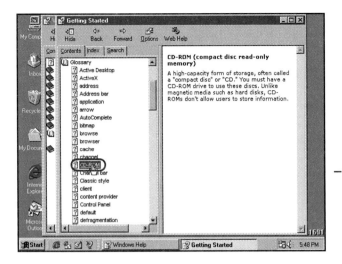

7 Scroll down and click the glossary term **CD-ROM**. Its definition appears on the right side.

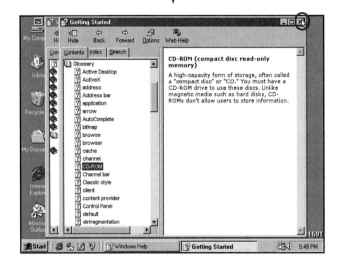

8 Close the **Getting Started** window by clicking the **Close** box on the upper-right corner of the window. The Windows Help window will still be on the desktop.

Task 2

Locating a Topic Using the Index Feature

Why would I do this?

When using the Contents feature of Help, you are restricted to getting help on a broad range of topics that are presented. However, with the *Index* feature of Help, you can type a specific word or words on which to search for help. Topics listed in the index are in alphabetical order; additionally, there are many more topics listed in the index than in the Contents tab of the Help Topics dialog box.

In this task, you learn how to use the Index tab in the Help Topics dialog box.

1 Click the **Index** tab in the Help Topics dialog box. A list of alphabetized Help topics appears.

In Depth: At first, the index may not appear alphabetized because the first items in the list don't begin with the letter "a." However, items such as .bmp files and 16-color display appear on the list because they are first in the "collating sequence" (the way the computer alphabetizes things). If you scroll down the list, you will see the rest of the items as you are used to seeing them alphabetized.

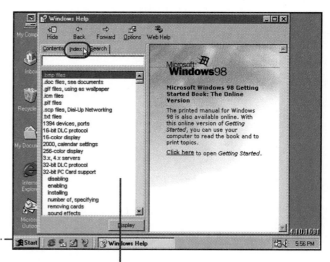

Alphabetized list of topics

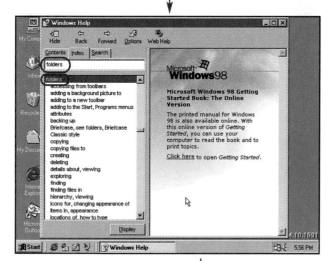

2 A blinking cursor appears in the text box at the top of the tab. Type **folders** to find help on this topic. As you type, the list jumps to the topic for which you are searching.

Quick Tip: You can scroll through the list of topics in the Index tab using the scrollbar to the right of the list box.

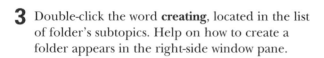

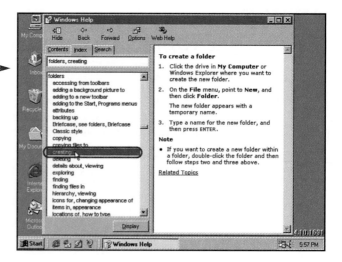

3 Double-click the word **creating**, located in the list of folder's subtopics. Help on how to create a folder appears in the right-side window pane.

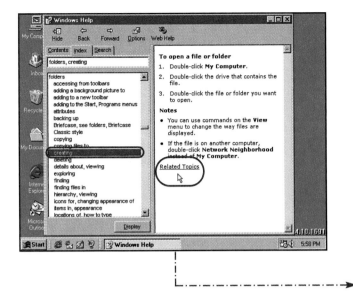

4 In the right-side window pane, click **Related Topics**. Help appears on topics related to creating a folder.

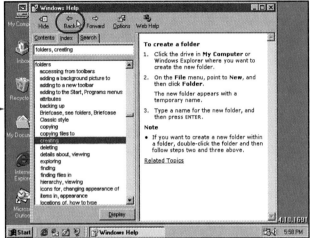

5 Click the **Back** button to return to the previous help screen.

Task 3

Locating a Topic Using the Find Feature

Why would I do this?

The Windows Help Topic called *Search* enables you to search for specific words within the Help topics.

In this task, you learn how to use the Find feature to look up information about using the Recycle Bin.

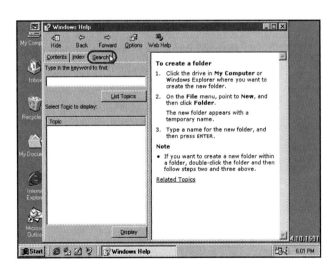

1 If necessary, click the **Search** tab in the Windows Help dialog box.

2 In the **Type in the keyword to find** text box, type **recycle** as shown in the figure.

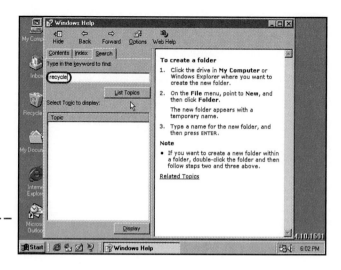

3 Click the **List Topics** command button. A list of all help topics containing the word "recycle" appears.

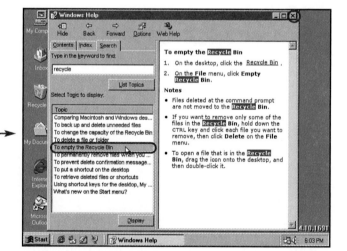

4 Double-click the topic **To empty the Recycle Bin**. Help on emptying the recycle bin appears on the right side with the keyword "recycle" highlighted.

In Depth: Instead of double-clicking a topic, you can select it and then click the **Display** command button.

Quick Tip: If you want to return to the desktop from Windows Help, simply click the **Close** window button.

Task 4

Printing a Help Topic

Why would I do this?

Windows 98 Help is set up so that you can read and implement instructions from a Help window and the window will stay on top of other windows while you work. Even with this convenience, sometimes it's easier to print a Help topic for future reference than it is to read it from the screen. You can choose a topic in the Help window and print it quickly and easily.

In this task, you learn how to print a Help topic.

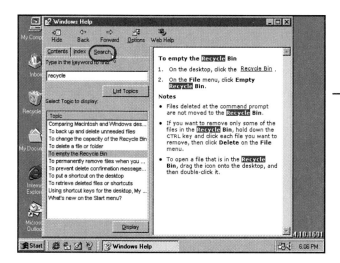

1 If it is not already selected, click the **Search** tab in the Help Topics dialog box.

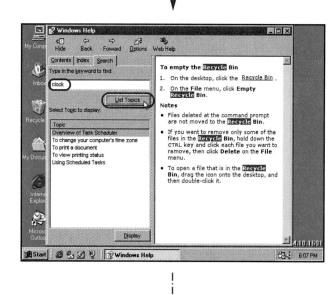

2 Type **clock** in the **Type in the keyword to find:** text box and then click the **List Topics** command button.

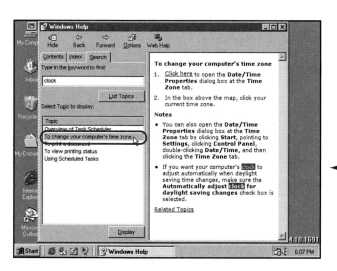

3 From the topics list, double-click **To change your computer's time zone**. Help appears on the right side.

4 From the toolbar near the top of the window, click the **Options** button. A series of options drops down.

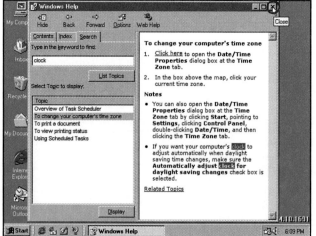

Pothole: If your printer is not properly connected or is not turned on, a dialog box will appear warning you of this when you attempt to print. Therefore, before printing, make sure that you do indeed have a printer connected to your PC and that it is turned on.

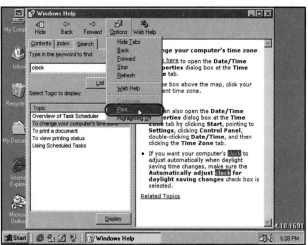

5 Click the **Print** menu choice to print the topic. In the Print dialog box, click **OK**.

6 Click the **Close** button in the Windows Help window to return to the desktop.

Task 5

Using Context-Sensitive Help

Why would I do this?

When using dialog boxes, Windows 98 includes an additional Help feature called *What's This?*, which is represented by a question mark in the window's title bar. To use this feature, click the question mark. The mouse pointer turns into a pointer with a question mark. You can then point to the dialog box feature you need help on, click it, and voila!—you now have context-sensitive help.

In this task, you learn how to use the *What's This?* feature.

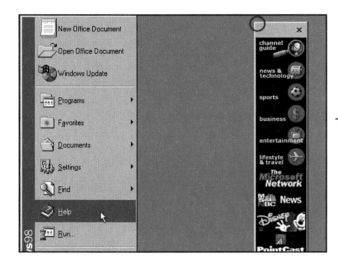

1 From the **Start** menu, choose **Settings** and then **Folder Options**. The Folder Options dialog box is displayed. Notice the question mark icon in the top-right corner of the dialog box.

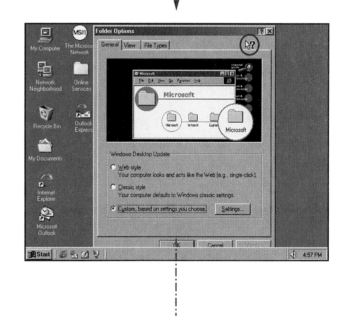

2 Click the **question mark**. The mouse pointer changes to a pointer with a question mark.

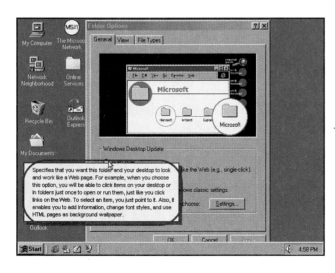

3 Click the **Web Style** option button. A help box is displayed describing the option. The mouse pointer returns to its usual form.

4 After reading the explanation, click any empty area on the desktop to close the context-sensitive help. Choose the **Classic Style** option by clicking its option button.

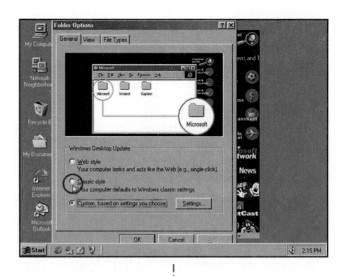

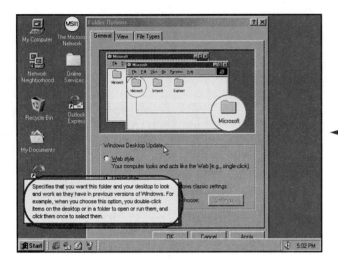

5 Press F1 on the top row of your keyboard to get a context-sensitive description of this option. F1 acts as a shortcut to context-sensitive help. This is particularly helpful in cases where the question mark (?) button isn't available.

6 Click the **Cancel** button to close the window without making any changes to your settings.

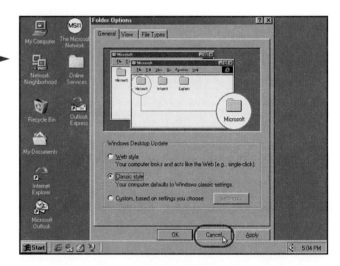

Task 6

Getting Help on the Web

Why would I do this?

Even with all the help available in Windows 98, you'll eventually have a problem that cannot be solved through local resources. In such a case, the next step is to seek help on the Web. Microsoft maintains a Web site that offers a wide variety of help options and customer support.

In this task, you learn how to access Windows 98 Help on the Web.

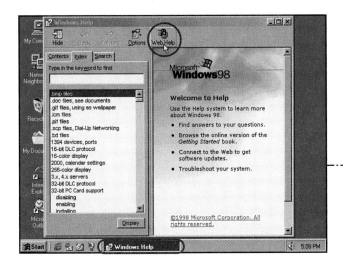

1 From the **Start** menu, choose **Help**. The Help program is displayed in a window on the desktop. Click the **Web Help** button on the toolbar.

2 An explanation of Microsoft's Support Online is displayed in the right help window. Scroll down and click the **Support Online** link at the end of the explanation.

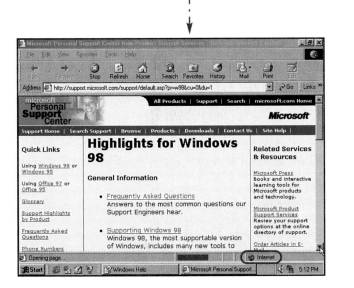

3 Internet Explorer opens and connects to Microsoft's Windows 98 Web page. Scroll through the information on the page. Feel free to explore links.

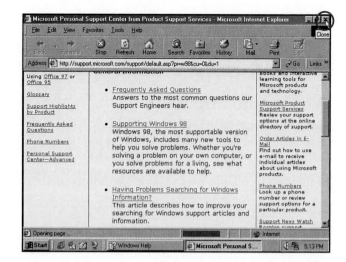

4 Close **Internet Explorer**. We'll learn more about the Web and Internet Explorer in Lesson 8. Close **Windows Help**.

Student Exercises

True-False

For each of the following, circle either T or F to indicate whether the statement is true or false.

T   F   **1.** Hyperprint is text that links one document to other related documents.

T   F   **2.** You can print a Help topic by choosing **Print** from the **Options** menu.

T   F   **3.** The book icons appear in the **Contents** section of the Windows Help window.

T   F   **4.** A book icon can be expanded (or contracted) by double-clicking it.

T   F   **5.** The *What's This?* feature is represented by a question mark.

T   F   **6.** Context-sensitive help is found by clicking the **What's This?** button, then the object in question.

T   F   **7.** For the most up-to-date help information, click the **Web Help** button.

T   F   **8.** Help can be found on any icon, button, or object on the screen by right-clicking it.

T   F   **9.** The **Contents** Help page offers more detailed help than the **Index** page.

T   F   **10.** The **Search** Help page allows you to search all Help pages for a keyword of your choice.

Identifying Parts of the Windows 98 Screen

Refer to the figure and identify the numbered parts of the screen. Write the letter of the correct label in the space next to the number.

1. _____
2. _____
3. _____
4. _____
5. _____
6. _____
7. _____
8. _____
9. _____
10. _____

A. What's This?

B. Hypertext

C. All Help Topics listed alphabetically

D. General Help categories listed here

E. A Help Search tool

F. To the Microsoft Web site

G. Glossary term

H. Selected Help Topic

I. Contains unseen subcategories

J. Go here to print

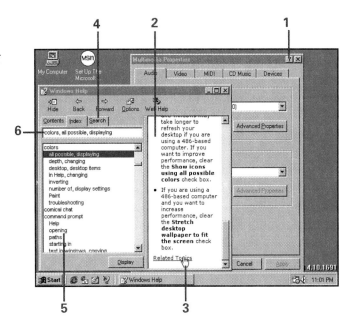

Matching

Match the statements below to the word or phrase that is the best match from the list. Write the letter of the matching word or phrase in the space provided next to the number.

1. ___ If you click this in a dialog box and then click an item within the dialog box, you will see a brief definition of the item that you clicked.

2. ___ This type of help provides assistance at the PC, eliminating or reducing the need for printed manuals.

3. ___ This text, when clicked, opens a related document.

4. ___ If you know the topic name on which you seek help, use this Help page.

5. ___ General Help Topics can be found on this page.

6. ___ If you are unable to find the information you need within the Help documents, you try clicking this button.

7. ___ To view help information on a given topic, double click the topic in the menu or high-light it and click this button.

8. ___ If you wish to see every reference to a given topic you would go to this Help page.

9. ___ These underlined words will be defined when clicked.

10. ___ Help can be accessed quickly from this location.

A. Hypertext

B. What's This?

C. Index

D. Contents

E. Glossary term

F. Start menu

G. Online Help

H. Web Help

I. Display

J. Find

Reinforcement Exercises

Exercise 1

1. Start Help from the Start menu.

2. Go to the Glossary by choosing **Contents/Getting Started Book/Microsoft Windows 98 Getting Started**, clicking **Click here** in the right window and **Glossary** in the new window.

3. Look up the terms **Address bar**, **Web Browser** and **menu** in the glossary.

4. Close the **Getting Started** window.

Exercise 3

1. From the Start menu, choose **Settings**, then **Taskbar**. Using "What's This?" help, find out what the A<u>u</u>to hide option does.

Exercise 5

1. Use Web Help (Support Online) to skim through the Windows 98 How-To Guide.

Exercise 2

1. With the Contents tab already selected, double-click **What's New in Windows 98**.

2. Under the **More entertaining and fun** subtopic, find out about **Web TV for Windows**.

3. Print the **Help Topic**.

Exercise 4

1. Using the Help glossary, find the definition for wallpaper.

2. Click the **Search** tab in the Windows Help window.

3. Find information on how to change the wallpaper on your desktop.

4. Print the **Help Topic**.

Lesson 6
Using Windows Accessories

Task 1: Writing and Editing in WordPad

Task 2: Using Paint

Task 3: Controlling Multimedia by Playing Sounds

Task 4: Controlling Multimedia by Playing Movies

Task 5: Scanning For and Fixing Disk Errors

Introduction

Windows has several useful Accessories (or programs) you can use in your work. These Accessories are not full-blown programs, but they are useful for specific jobs in the Windows environment. Included in the Accessories are a painting program, a program to detect and fix errors on your disk, a modest word processing program, multimedia players, and other practical applications.

In this lesson, you work with four Windows Accessories: Paint, WordPad, Media Player, ActiveMovie Control, and ScanDisk.

Visual Summary

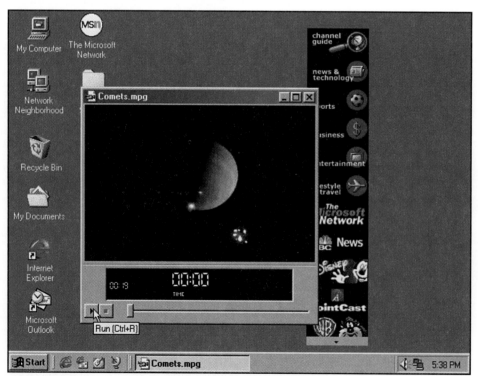

When you are done with Task 4, you will have a Windows 98 desktop that looks like this:

Task 1

Writing and Editing in WordPad

Why would I do this?

You can use WordPad to edit or read text files or to quickly create formatted text such as notes, memos, and fax sheets. WordPad saves files in Word 6 format by default, but you can save files in other formats too.

In this task, you learn to enter text in WordPad.

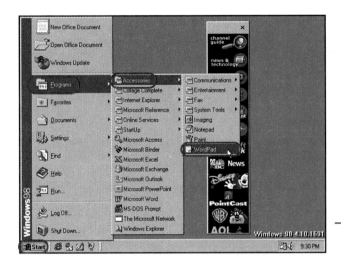

1 Make sure that the student CD-ROM is placed in the CD-ROM drive and that your student data disk is in drive A. Click the **Start** button and select **Programs**, **Accessories**, and then click **WordPad** from the menu bars. The WordPad program launches.

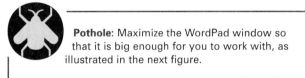

Pothole: Maximize the WordPad window so that it is big enough for you to work with, as illustrated in the next figure.

2 Type your first name and press ↵Enter. Then type your address on the next two lines. Use the figure as a guideline.

Pothole: If you make a typing mistake, press the Backspace key to delete one character at a time. Or, select the text to delete with the mouse, then press the Delete key to erase it.

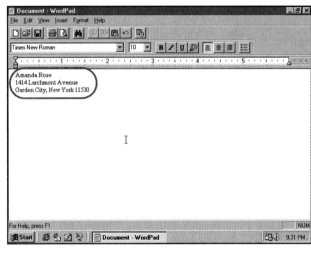

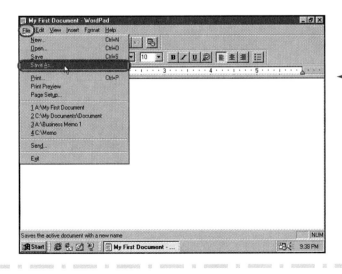

3 Save your work by selecting **File**, **Save As** from the menu bar.

In Depth: If you want to type paragraphs of text, you do not need to press ↵Enter at the end of a line to start a new line. WordPad includes automatic text wrap; you only press ↵Enter to start a new paragraph.

4 The Save As dialog box opens. Click the down arrow next to the **Save in** list box and **select 3 ½ Floppy (A:)** as the disk location to save the file.

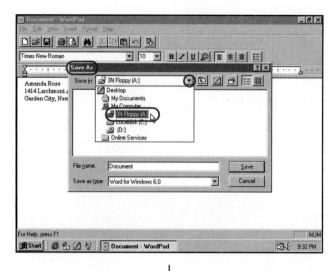

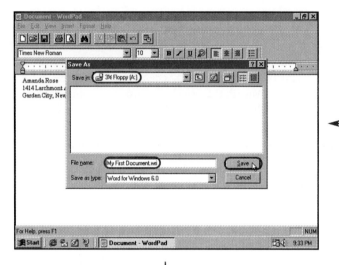

5 In the **File name** text box, type **My First Document** as the file name and click the **Save** button. The file is saved to the disk in drive A:.

Print button

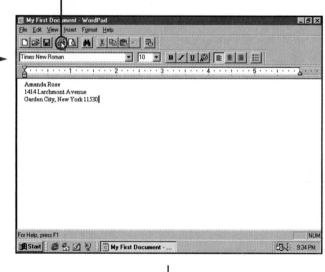

6 Click the **Print** button.

Pothole: Make sure that your printer is turned on and ready to print.

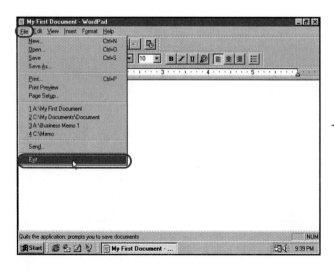

7 Close the **WordPad** program.

Task 2

Using Paint

Why would I do this?

Use Paint to create art and to edit graphics such as clip art, scanned art, and art files from other programs. You can add lines, shapes, and colors to your creation.

In this task, you learn how to create a graphic and edit a graphic file using Paint.

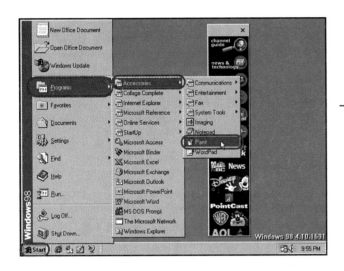

1 Click the **Start** button and then select **Programs**, **Accessories**, and then click **Paint**.

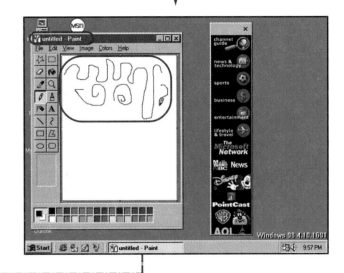

2 The Paint window opens. Click the **pencil tool** on the toolbox on the left side of the Paint window; then drag it around on the drawing surface to get the feel for freehand drawing.

> **Pothole:** Your first drawing using Paint will probably not be a masterpiece, so don't worry if you make a mistake. Right now, you just want to get used to using Paint's drawing tools.

3 Click **File**, **New** from the menu bar to erase your painting. Click **No** when prompted to save your changes.

> **Quick Tip:** You can also click in the color palette at the bottom of the Paint window to choose a color other than black to use with the selected tool.

> **In Depth:** You can cancel the last figure drawn by pulling down the Edit menu and selecting Undo. You can delete parts of a drawing by picking the eraser tool from the tool box and "erasing" parts of your drawing.

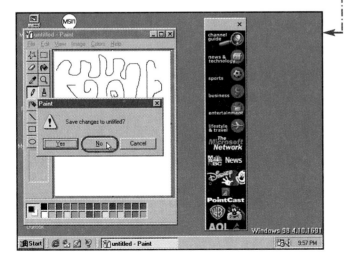

4 Click the **rectangle tool** on the lower-left side of the Paint toolbox. Place the pointer on the drawing surface where you want the upper-left corner of the rectangle to begin. Drag the tool down and to the right. When you release the mouse, the rectangle is drawn. This click-and-drag method applies for most of the drawing tools.

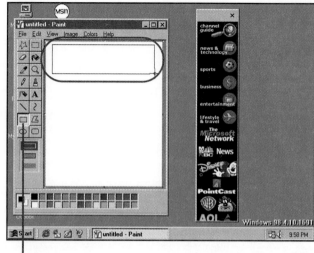

Quick Tip: If you don't know the name of a tool, place the mouse pointer on the middle of the tool and leave it there for a moment, a ScreenTip displays the name of the tool.

Rectangle tool

Select button

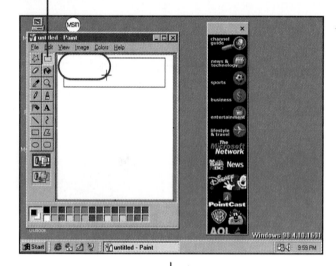

5 Click the **Select** button located on the upper right-hand corner of the Paint toolbox. Click and drag the cross-shaped pointer across part of your drawing. The tool creates a rectangle as you drag, and anything within the rectangle is selected. Press the Del key to remove the selected part of the drawing.

Quick Tip: You can also use the select tool to move and edit the selection.

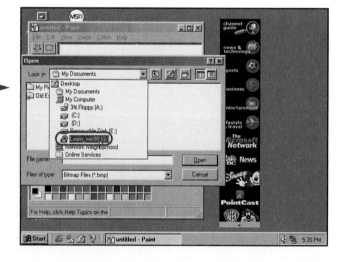

6 To edit an existing graphic file using Paint, you must first open it. Select **File,** and click **Open** from the menu bar. From the **Look in:** list box, pull down the list and select the location of your CD-ROM drive.

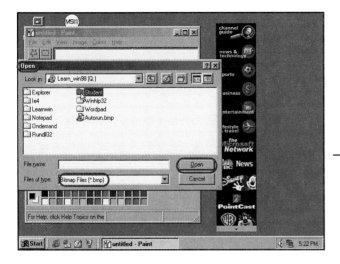

7 The Open dialog box opens. In the File name text box, type **circles.bmp** and click the **Open** button. When asked, "Save changes to untitled?" click **No**.

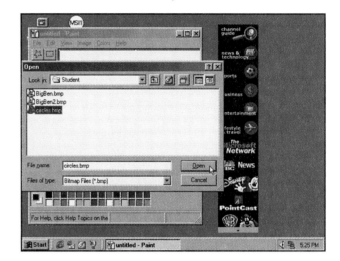

8 The **Paint** window opens with the circles image. Experiment with the toolbox and color palette to add to this image to create your own work of art.

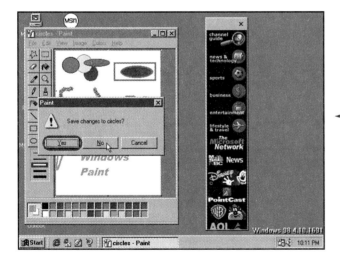

9 When you finish the drawing, click the **Close** box on the title bar. Click **Yes** when prompted to save your work and save it to your student data disk.

Task 3

Controlling Multimedia by Playing Sounds

Why would I do this?

Windows 98 is chock full of new Multimedia features. It gives you the ability to record and play sounds, view movies and other video, listen to CDs, and, if you have the right hardware, you can even watch TV on your personal computer. In this lesson, you'll see just a fraction of the multimedia capabilities available on Windows 98.

In this task, you learn how to use the Media Player to play a sound.

1 Click **Start** and then select **Programs**, **Accessories**, **Entertainment**, and then click **Media Player** from the menu. The **Media Player** window opens.

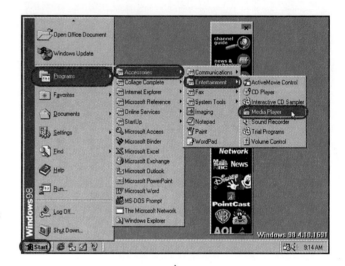

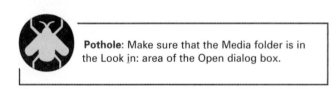

2 Select **File**, **Open** from the Media Player menu bar. The Open dialog box opens.

Pothole: Make sure that the Media folder is in the Look in: area of the Open dialog box.

3 Scroll (if necessary) through the list box until you find **The Microsoft Sound** file. Click it and then click the **Open** button.

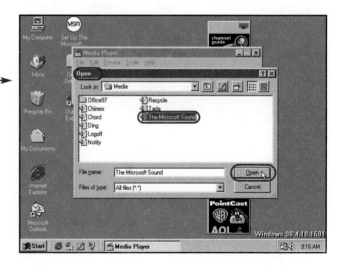

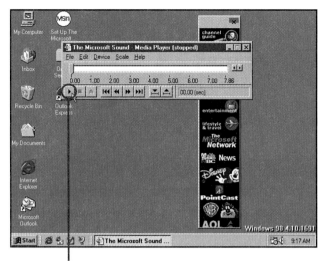

Play button

4 At the bottom of the Media Player is a series of buttons that look like VCR buttons. Click the **Play** button. If you have speakers or earphones attached to your computer, you should hear the sound.

In Depth: You can stop the sound while it is playing, slow it down, speed it up, and adjust other settings with the menu commands and buttons.

5 Click the **Close** button to close the Media Player window.

In Depth: You can use the Media Player to play music CDs, but if you use the CD Player accessory instead, it offers many more features designed specifically for playing CDs.

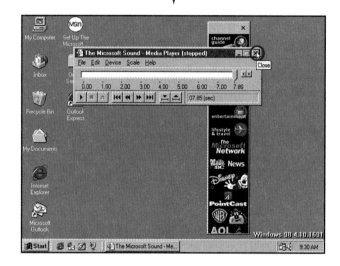

Task 4

Controlling Multimedia by Playing Movies

Why would I do this?

Windows 98 delivers high-performance multimedia capabilities. In addition to adding a new dimension to your business tasks, you can also use your PC as a fun, state-of-the-art entertainment center.

In this task, you learn how to use the ActiveMovie Control to play a movie.

1 Click **Start** and then select **Programs**, **Accessories**, **Entertainment**, and then click **ActiveMovie Control**. The Open dialog box opens.

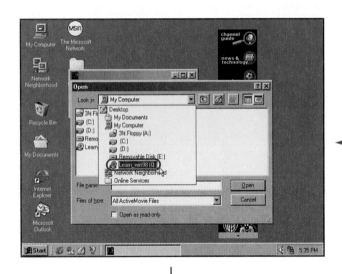

2 In the Look in: list box, select the **CD-ROM drive**. A list of available movies appears.

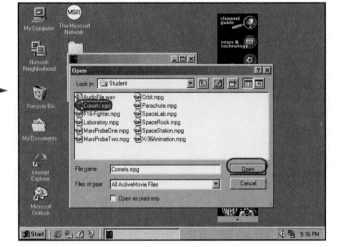

3 Click the file **Comet.mpg** and then click the **Open** button. The ActiveMovie Control window opens.

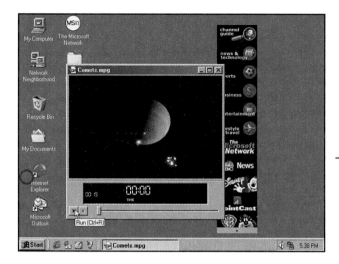

4 On the lower-left side of the window is a VCR button with an arrow on it. Click it to play the 30-second movie.

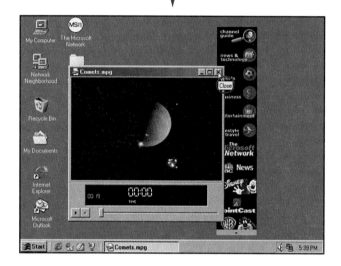

5 When the movie has completed playing, close the **Comet** window by clicking the **Close** box on the upper-right side of the window.

In Depth: Windows 98 also gives you the capability to play regular music CDs with the CD Player, view and edit photos, and if you have the right hardware, you can even select and play cable television programs.

Task 5

Scanning For and Fixing Disk Errors

Why would I do this?

If you have a damaged disk, Windows may display an error message when you try to open or save a file, or you may notice lost or disarrayed data in some of your files. You can scan the disk for damage and perhaps retrieve the data before you lose it all using the *ScanDisk* program.

In this task, you learn how to use ScanDisk to check your hard drive for errors.

1 Click **Start** and then select **Programs**, **Accessories**, **System Tools**, and click **ScanDisk**. The Scandisk program launches.

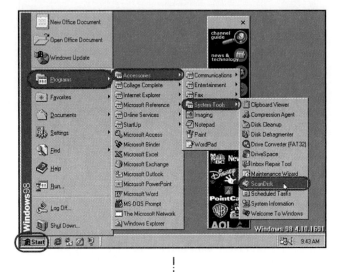

Pothole: If your system has more disk drives than what appears in the figure, you may have to scroll through the list to select the C: drive.

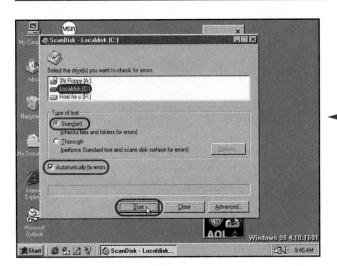

2 In the ScanDisk dialog box, click the **C:** drive in the Select the dri_v_e(s) you want to check for errors: area. Also click the **Standard** option button. Check mark the Automatically fix errors check box. Click the **Start** button to begin scanning the disk for errors and have any fixed, if they exist.

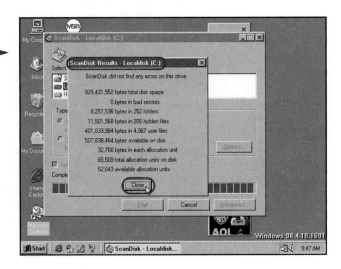

3 When the scan is complete, a report opens in the **ScanDisk Results** window. Read the report, then click the **Close** button to exit the window.

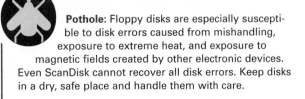
Pothole: Floppy disks are especially susceptible to disk errors caused from mishandling, exposure to extreme heat, and exposure to magnetic fields created by other electronic devices. Even ScanDisk cannot recover all disk errors. Keep disks in a dry, safe place and handle them with care.

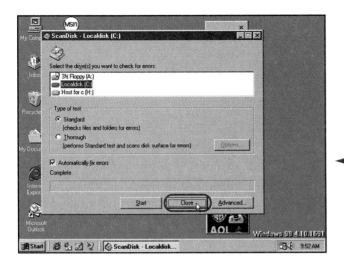

4 Click the **Close** button in the ScanDisk window to return to the desktop.

Student Exercises

True-False

For each of the following, circle T or F to indicate whether the statement is true or false.

T F **1.** All of the Windows Accessories programs are full-fledged, comprehensive applications that can handle virtually any task within its area.

T F **2.** In WordPad, press the [Del] key to erase any characters immediately to the left of the insertion point.

T F **3.** The interface of the Media Player window resembles a VCR control panel.

T F **4.** Files created in the Media Player window may be used by other accessories.

T F **5.** The ActiveMovie control can also be used to edit and manipulate photos.

T F **6.** Floppy disks are exceptionally durable. They can be subjected to rough handling, exposure, and to extreme environmental conditions.

T F **7.** The editing of ClipArt and scanned images is most appropriately done with the Paint accessory.

T F **8.** ScanDisk is extremely competent in detecting and repairing virtually any disk error.

T F **9.** The Zoom command in Paint is used to make the image being edited a large size.

T F **10.** One of ScanDisk's primary functions is to easily and quickly format disks.

Identifying Parts of the Windows 98 Screen

Refer to the figure and identify the numbered parts of the screen. Write the letter of the correct label in the space next to the number.

1. _____
2. _____
3. _____
4. _____
5. _____
6. _____
7. _____
8. _____
9. _____
10. _____

A. VCR Buttons

B. Color Palette

C. Toolbox

D. Media Player

E. Select Tool

F. WordPad

G. Eraser Tool

H. Cursor

I. Paint

J. I-Beam Pointer

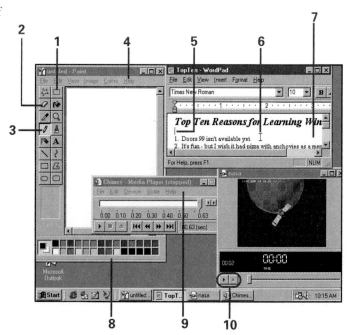

Matching

Match the statements below to the word or phrase that is the best match from the list. Write the letter of the matching word or phrase in the space provided next to the number.

1. ___ This is used to select colors for objects created with the Paint accessory.

2. ___ Short notes and items like fax cover sheets are best created with this accessory.

3. ___ An audio, video, or sound file is considered to be this type of file.

4. ___ A type of image that can be created, edited, and used for wallpaper.

5. ___ This is the name of the accessory that is used to fix disk errors.

6. ___ ScanDisk is located under this submenu of the Accessories menu.

7. ___ Media Player is located under this submenu of the Accessories menu.

8. ___ This part of the Paint program contains the objects that you can use to draw shapes and figures, erase, select, magnify, and color objects on the drawing area.

9. ___ To start a new paragraph in WordPad, press this key.

10. ___ Both WordPad and Paint are located directly under this menu.

A. System Tools menu

B. Toolbox

C. Accessories menu

D. FixDisk

E. Bitmap

F. Entertainment menu

G. Multimedia

H. ◆Shift + Ctrl

I. ScanDisk

J. ↵Enter

K. Color Palette

L. WordPad

Reinforcement Exercises

Exercise 1

1. Create a letterhead with the Paint accessory to look similar to the figure below:

2. Save the file as **Letterhead** on your student data disk.

3. Print the image.

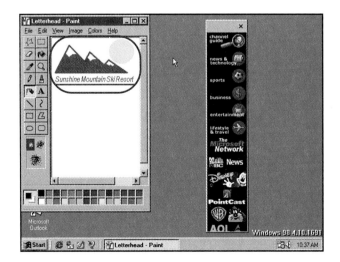

Exercise 2

1. In **WordPad**, create and print the following document.

2. Save the file as **Meeting Memo** on your student data disk.

Exercise 4

1. On your CD-ROM is a sound file called **midimusic**. Play it.

2. Using the ActiveMovie Control, play the movie files **X-36Animation**, **SpaceRock**, and **MarsProbeOne**.

Exercise 3

1. Scan a blank floppy disk for errors. Make sure that a standard type of test is done. All errors are to be corrected automatically.

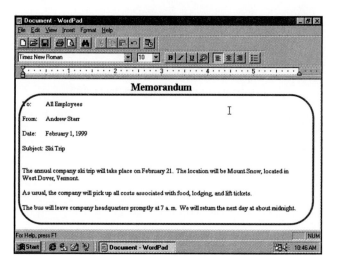

Exercise 5

1. Revise the **Meeting Memo** document to add the following sentence at the end of the the first paragraph: **He will be accompanied by his assistant, Gary Matthews.**

2. Delete the last paragraph and add this paragraph: **Refreshments will be served at the meeting.**

3. Save the document, then print it.

Lesson 7
Sharing Data with Windows

Task 1 Switching Between Applications

Task 2 Copying Data Between Applications

Task 3 Moving a Graphic Image Between Applications

Task 4 Linking Data Between Applications

Introduction

One of the biggest advantages of using Windows and Windows applications is that you can easily and efficiently share data—text, figures, pictures, sounds, lists, and so on—between applications. Whether you are working with word processing documents, spreadsheets, databases, or drawing programs, you can share data among all of your Windows applications.

In this lesson, you learn how to switch between applications and share data by copying, moving, and embedding.

Visual Summary

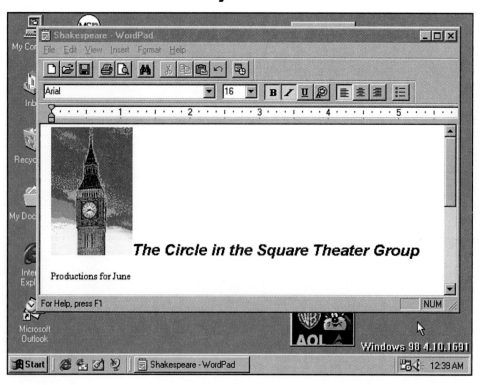

When you are done with Task 4, you will have a Windows 98 desktop that looks like this:

Task 1

Switching Between Applications

Why would I do this?

You switch between applications in order to complete work more efficiently and effectively. Switching between applications enables you to share and compare data and to update and complete work faster and easier.

In this task, you learn how to switch back and forth between WordPad and Paint.

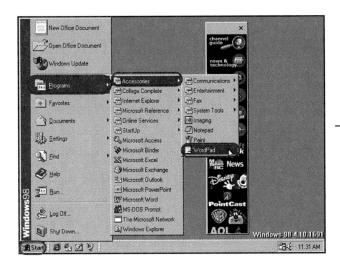

1 Click **Start**, select **Programs**, **Accessories**, and then click **WordPad**.

2 Click the **Minimize** button on the WordPad title bar. WordPad remains as a button on the taskbar.

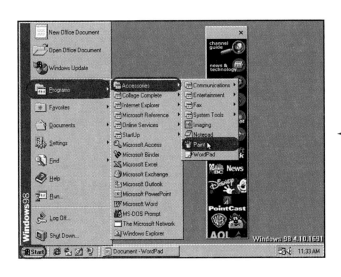

3 Click **Start**, select **Programs**, **Accessories**, and then click **Paint** to launch the Paint program.

4 To switch back to the WordPad program, click the **WordPad** button on the taskbar. Windows brings the WordPad program to the foreground. The Paint program is running in the background.

Quick Tip: You can also make a program active and appear in the foreground by clicking anywhere in its window.

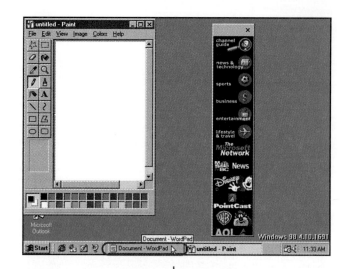

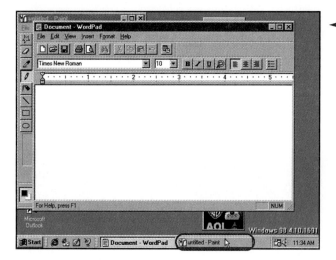

5 To switch back to the Paint program, click the **Paint** button on the taskbar.

Quick Tip: You can also switch back and forth between two programs by using the Alt + Tab method. While holding down Alt, keep pressing Tab until the program that you want to work with is selected. Release Alt to switch to the selected program.

Task 2

Copying Data Between Applications

Why would I do this?

You can *copy* data from a document in one application and *paste* it into another document in another application. This saves you time by eliminating the need to recreate the data. In addition to text, you can copy many objects, including spreadsheets, figures, charts, and clip art.

In this task, you learn how to copy a graphic image from Paint to WordPad.

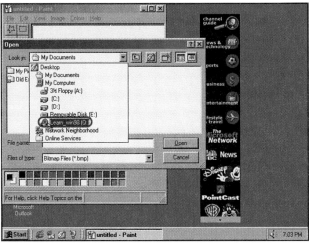

1 Make sure that the Learn Windows 98 CD-ROM is in the CD-ROM drive. In the Paint program that is active on your desktop, pull down the **File** menu, select **Open**, pull down the **Look in:** list box, and select the CD-ROM drive.

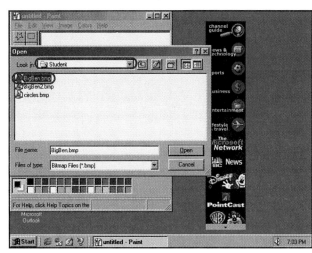

2 Double-click the **Student** folder, then double-click **BigBen** from the list of files presented in the dialog box. A picture of the famous clock tower appears in the Paint drawing area.

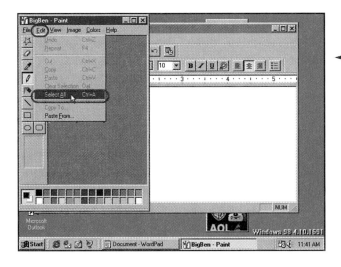

3 Pull down the **Edit** menu and click **Select All**. The entire picture of Big Ben is selected.

4 Pull down the **Edit** menu and then select **Copy**. A copy of the image is placed on the *Clipboard*.

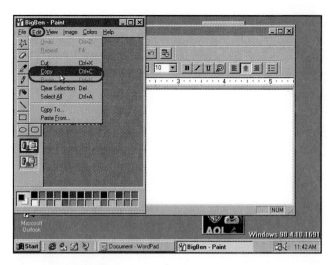

Quick Tip: In Paint, you can select part of an image if you use the Select tool instead of using Select All from the menu.

5 Click the **WordPad** program button on the taskbar and enter the text, as shown in the figure: The famous 320 foot tower that rises above England's Houses of Parliament was actually named after Sir Benjamin Hall, the Chief Commissioner of Works in 1858.

The deep chimes of the bell within the tower have become a symbol of Britain worldwide.

(Note: See the In-Depth note below if you need assistance in formatting the text for bold and italic.)

6 Place the Mouse pointer to the left of the word **Big** in the first line and click the mouse button once. This places the blinking cursor (Insertion Point) to the left of the word **Big** and marks the place where the object will be placed.

InDepth: When applying special formatting to text, such as italic or boldface, first enter all of the text. To boldface, highlight the text to boldface, then click the **Bold** button on the Formatting toolbar, shown in the figure. To italicize, select the text to italicize, then click the Italic button on the Formatting toolbar, shown in the figure. Click both buttons again to deselect them.

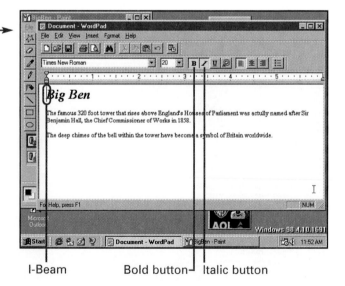

I-Beam   Bold button — Italic button

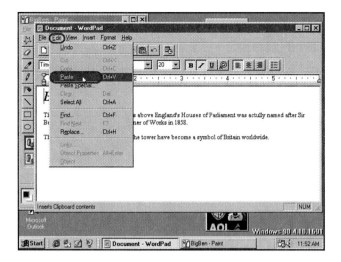

7 Choose **Edit**, **Paste** from the menu bar. The figure from the Paint program is pasted into the WordPad document before the word **Big** in the first line. Click outside the image to deselect it. Leave the WordPad and Paint programs open for use in the next Task.

In Depth: The image that was copied to the Clipboard remains in the Clipboard until another image is placed in the Clipboard or until the computer is turned off.

Task 3

Moving a Graphic Image Between Applications

Why would I do this?

You can move, or *cut*, information from one application to another. For example, you might want to move a picture that you have created with Paint to a document created with WordPad.

In this task, you learn how to move data between WordPad and Paint.

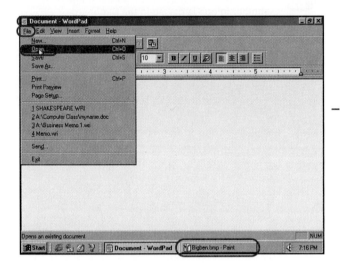

1 Make sure that the Learn Windows 98 CD is inserted into the CD-ROM drive. Choose **File**, **Open** from the WordPad menu bar.

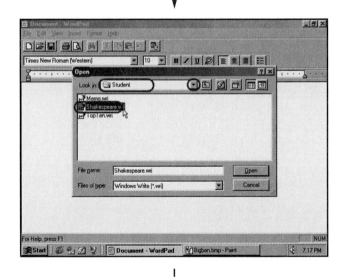

2 The Open dialog box appears. Click the list arrow next to the **Look in** text box and select the **CD-ROM drive**. Double-click the **Student** folder. From the **Files of type** pull down list, select **Windows Write (*.wri)**. Double-click **Shakespeare** from the list that appears in the dialog box.

3 Click **No** when prompted to save your changes. The Shakespeare WordPad document opens on the screen.

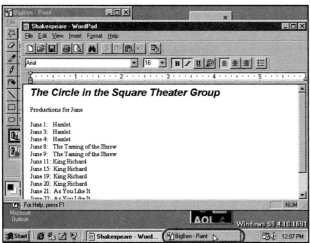
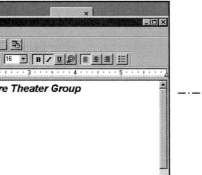

4 Click the **Paint** button on the taskbar to bring the Paint program to the foreground.

5 If the Big Ben image is not already selected, use the **Select** tool to select the picture. Choose **Edit, Cut** from the **Paint** menu bar. The source image is removed from the Paint program and is placed in the Clipboard.

6 Click the **WordPad** button on the taskbar.

7 The WordPad program comes to the foreground. Click to the left of the word "The" in the title. Choose **Edit**, **Paste** to move the picture from the clipboard to the WordPad program. Click elsewhere to deselect the image.

8 Click the **Paint** program button on the taskbar. Choose **File**, **Exit** from the **Paint** menu bar.

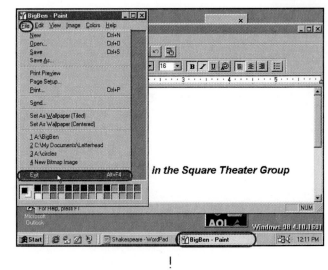

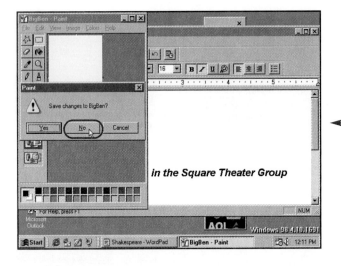

9 Click **No** when prompted to save your changes. The Paint file is not saved and the program closes.

Task 4

Linking Data Between Applications

Why would I do this?

At times, you may wish to edit data that you have *embedded* into another application. For instance, you may want to edit the Paint image of Big Ben once you have pasted it into your WordPad document.

In this task, you learn how to edit embedded data in documents.

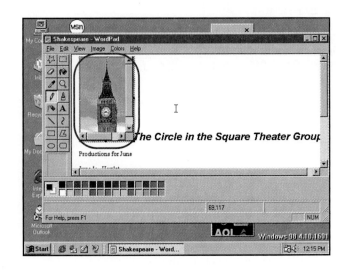

1 In the WordPad document, double-click the **Paint** image. The image is ready to be edited.

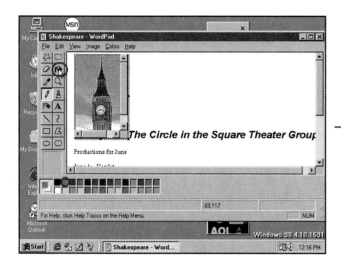

2 In the color palette at the bottom of the screen, select a gray color, then select the **Fill With Color** tool in the toolbox.

3 Click the background of the Paint image and it will fill with the color that you selected from the color palette. The more areas you click, the more areas will fill with color.

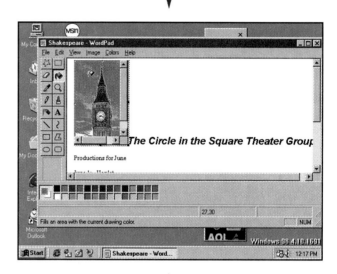

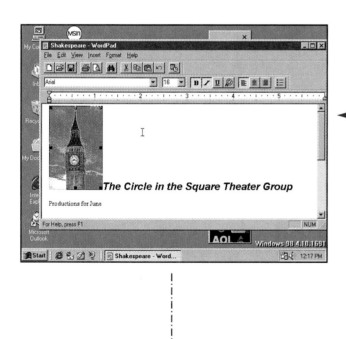

4 Click anywhere in the **WordPad** document to return to the WordPad program with the updated image.

5 Close the **WordPad** program. Click **No** when prompted to save your changes.

Student Exercises

True-False

For each of the following, check T or F to indicate whether the statement is true or false.

T   F   **1.** Data waiting to be pasted is stored on the clipboard.

T   F   **2.** In order to copy data from one application to another, both applications must be opened concurrently.

T   F   **3.** Clicking anywhere in a window will bring it to the foreground.

T   F   **4.** A window in the foreground is indicated by its dimmed title bar.

T   F   **5.** Data on the clipboard may be pasted repeatedly.

T   F   **6.** An embedded object may be edited using the toolbars and menus from the program used to create the object.

T   F   **7.** Sounds, spreadsheets, charts, and figures may be embedded in documents.

T   F   **8.** You must open the Clipboard prior to copying or pasting data to it.

T   F   **9.** WordPad and Paint are the only Windows programs that you can cut, copy, and paste between.

T   F   **10.** The Cut command actually removes the data from the document, whereas the Copy command does not.

Identifying Parts of the Windows 98 Screen

Refer to the figure and identify the numbered parts of the screen. Write the letter of the correct label in the space next to the number.

1. _____
2. _____
3. _____
4. _____
5. _____
6. _____
7. _____
8. _____
9. _____

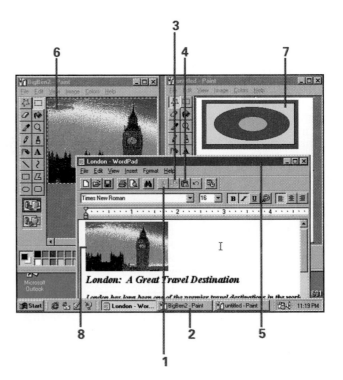

A. Cut button

B. Copy button

C. Paste button

D. Taskbar button

E. Active window

F. Selected Paintbrush Image

G. Unselected Paintbrush Image

H. Clipboard

I. Embedded Object

Matching

Match the statements below to the word or phrase that is the best match from the list. Write the letter of the matching word or phrase in the space provided next to the number.

1. ___ Use this shortcut for pasting data.

2. ___ This is the temporary holding area for data that has been cut or copied.

3. ___ The clipboard is a subsection of this.

4. ___ This command leaves the selected data intact while duplicating it on the clipboard.

5. ___ This command will remove data from an application and place it in the Clipboard.

6. ___ This is the action of placing an object from the clipboard into a document.

7. ___ Do this prior to copying or cutting.

8. ___ When pasting into a WordPad document, the data is pasted where this object is positioned.

9. ___ The Copy and Paste menu commands are located in this menu.

10. ___ Data from one document or application that has been copied or pasted into another application is referred to as this type of object.

A. Memory

B. Paste

C. Select

D. Cut

E. Copy

F. Edit

G. Clipboard

H. Embedded

I. Insertion Point

J. Ctrl + y

Reinforcement Exercises

Exercise 1

1. Open the **TopTen** file on the Learn Windows 98 CD.

2. Use the Paint application to create a document similar to the one in the figure.

3. Copy the **Paint image** into the WordPad document.

4. Save the document on your student floppy disk as **TopTen**.

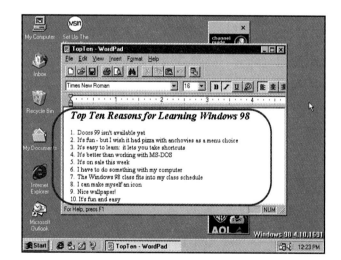

Exercise 2

1. Use WordPad to create a new document. If prompted, click **OK** to save the changes to TopTen.

2. In the new document, type **Study Windows 98 Now!!**

3. Cut the sentence and put it into your Paint program as shown in the figure below:

4. Close the **Paint** program. Click **No** when prompted to save your changes.

Exercise 3

1. Open the **TopTen** document in WordPad. Click **No** when prompted to save the changes to the other file.

2. Edit the Paint image by double-clicking it.

3. Change **My Top Ten List** in the embedded Paint image to **Why Learn Windows?**.

4. Change the color of the image to any color you wish.

5. Save your work and print the document.

6. Close the **WordPad** program to return to the desktop. Click **Yes** when prompted to save your changes.

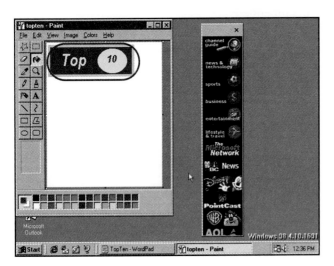

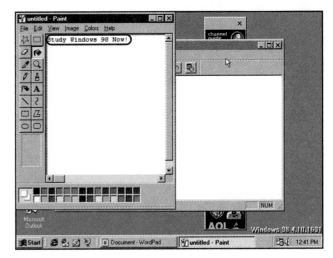

Lesson 8
Accessing the Internet

Introduction

Windows 98 is the first operating system designed to seamlessly integrate the Internet and World Wide Web into its interface. The resources that you access from Windows 98 menus and icons may be stored on your computer or on one of millions of other computers on the Internet. This new design effectively extends the boundaries of your computing experience to cover the entire world.

In this lesson, you learn the ways in which Windows 98 allows you to utilize the Internet.

Visual Summary

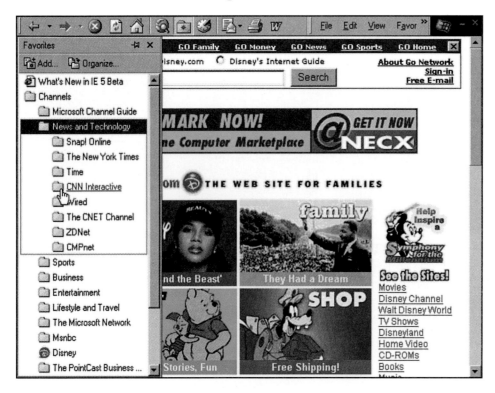

When you have completed Step 5 of Task 3, you will have a Windows 98 desktop that looks similar to this:

Task 1

Accessing the Web with Internet Explorer 4.0

Why would I do this?

A *network* is a collection of computers that are connected together to share software and hardware resources. Oftentimes, networks are interconnected to create larger networks. The largest of all interconnected networks is called the *Internet*. In the early 1990s, the Internet gained in popularity due to the birth of the World Wide Web. The World Wide Web, commonly called the *Web*, provides a graphical user interface and convenient methods by which to access Internet resources. The Web presents Internet documents as *Web pages*. Web pages can contain formatted text, images, forms, tables, sound and music, video, animation, program applications, and any object that can be digitally represented. You can move from Web page to Web page by clicking *hyperlinks*, often just called *links*. Links are marked objects and text within a Web page that act to interconnect related Web pages. Through the Web, users can access all types of files on millions of computers around the world.

Internet Explorer is a *Web Browser* program that allows you to view Web pages. This task acts as a basic introduction to the Web using Internet Explorer.

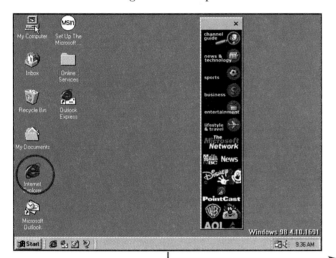

1 Double-click the **Internet Explorer** icon on the Windows 98 desktop or select it from the **Programs** menu.

Pothole: This lesson assumes that you have already set up your computer to connect to the Internet and are currently connected. If you have not yet set up an Internet connection, choose **Start**, **Programs**, **Accessories**, **Internet Tools**, **Connection Wizard**.

2 Click in the **Address** text box to highlight the text displayed there.

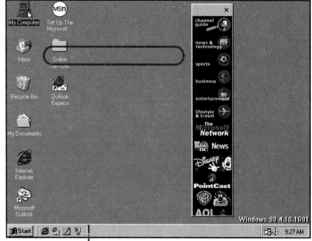

3 Type **www.snap.com** to replace the original address stored in the address box. Press ⏎Enter to connect to the Snap Web site.

In Depth: Web addresses are called *URLs* (Uniform Resource Locators). They start with **http://** and often include **www** and **.com**.

4 The Snap site offers news and information on local, national, and international levels. Scroll down the Web page until you find the **Computing & Internet** link. Click the words **Computing & Internet**.

Quick Tip: It is not necessary to type the **http://** of Web addresses. Your Web browser will make the assumption that this is necessary.

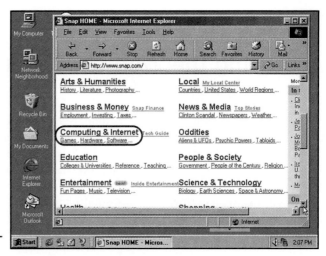

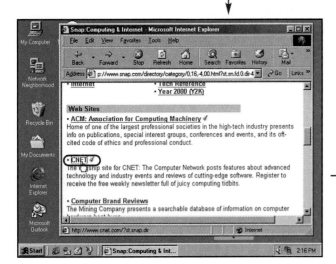

5 Browse through the information available on this page and then click the **CNET** link or type **http://www.cnet.com** in the **Address** box and press ↵Enter.

Pothole: Web sites are unpredictable. If you are unable to connect to Snap now, try again later.

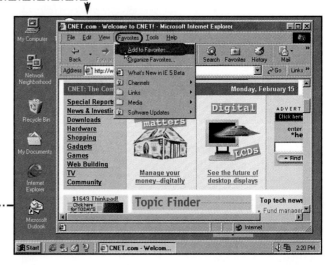

6 CNET offers technical information and reviews, software downloads, shopping, and lots more. Internet Explorer allows you to add your favorite Web sites to a list for easy future reference. Open Internet Explorer's **Favorites** menu and choose **Add to Favorites**.

7 Click **OK** to add CNET.com to your Favorites list.

8 Click the **Back** button on Internet Explorer's toolbar. The Back button takes you back to the previous Web page that you were viewing. Click it again to take you back to Snap's home page.

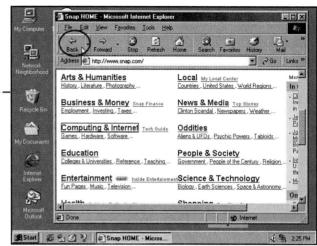

9 Click the **Favorites** button on Internet Explorer's toolbar.

10 Clicking the **Favorites** button displays your list of favorites in a window. Note that CNET.com is listed. Click the **CNET.com** reference in the list. The CNET Web page is displayed in the right window.

Quick Tip: The Favorites list comes preloaded with a number of good references in the **Links** and **Media** folder.

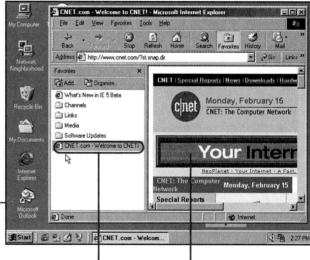

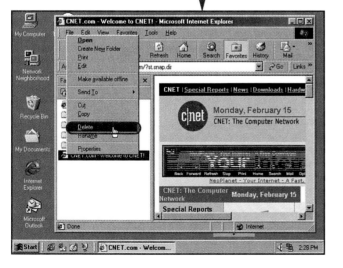

CNET link   CNET Web page

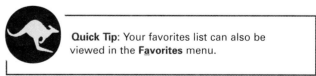

Quick Tip: Your favorites list can also be viewed in the **Favorites** menu.

11 Right-click the **CNET.com** link in your list of favorites and click **Delete** in the shortcut menu.

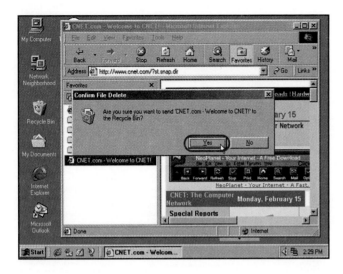

12 Confirm the deletion by clicking the **Yes** button. Close the **Internet Explorer** program.

> **Quick Tip:** The Favorites menu is also accessible from the Start menu and other Windows utility programs such as **My Computer** and **Windows Explorer**.

Task 2

Using Find to Search the Internet

Why would I do this?

Windows 98 blurs the distinction between accessing information from your own computer and from the Internet. A prime example of this is the **Find** option in the Start menu. **Find** allows you to look for files and folders on your own computer, or topics and people on the Internet.

The Internet has millions of Web sites that hold a seemingly limitless number of topics. Users need tools to help siphon through this data to find useful information for a current need. Windows 98 provides access to a number of such helpful tools.

Got some old friends with whom you've lost touch? Not sure where they live or how to get in touch? If they have an Internet account, there's a good chance that you can track them down with one of the search engines provided in Windows 98 for people on the Internet.

This lesson demonstrates how to use **Find** to search for information and people on the Internet.

1 From the Windows 98 **Start** menu, select **Find**, followed by **On the Internet**.

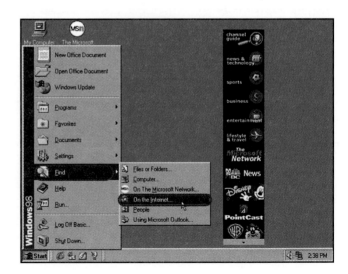

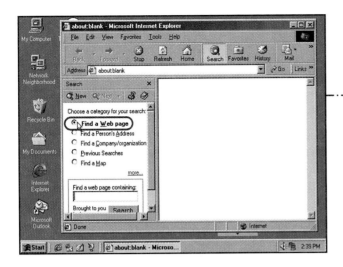

2 The Internet Explorer program opens with a list of options displayed in the **Search** window. The **Find a Web page** option is currently selected.

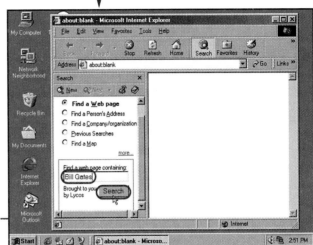

3 In the Search text box, type **Bill Gates**. Click the **Search** button.

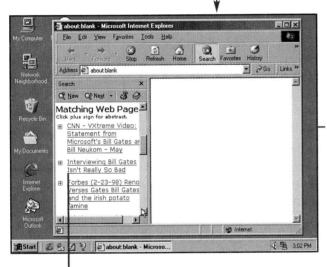

Links to pages that contain "Bill Gates"

4 The default *Search Engine* scours the Web for Web pages that contain references to Bill Gates. A list of such Web pages is displayed in the **Search** window.

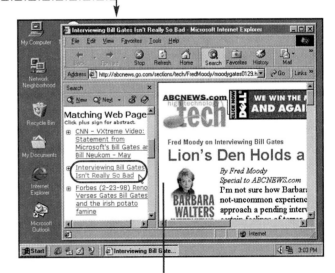

Related Web Page

5 Scroll down the list of links and click one that looks interesting. The related Web page is displayed in the right window.

In Depth: To see a list of the available search engines, click the down arrow button on the Search window's toolbar.

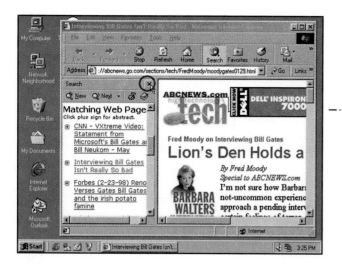

6 Close the Search window in Internet Explorer by clicking its **Close** button. Close **Internet Explorer**.

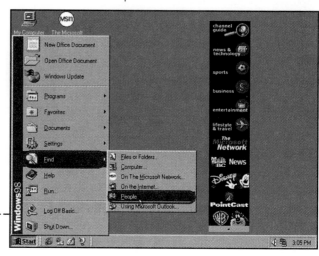

7 From the Windows 98 **Start** menu, select **Find**, **People**.

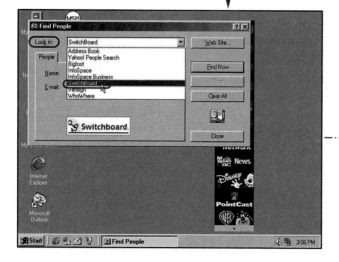

8 The Find People dialog box opens on the desktop. Choose **SwitchBoard** from the **Look in** drop-down list box.

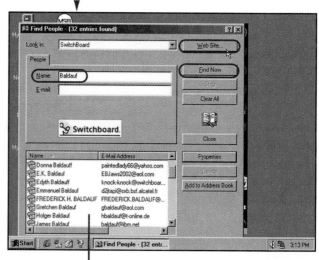

9 Type your last name in the **Name** textbox. Leave the **E-mail** text box empty and click the **Find Now** button. A list of all users who share your last name is displayed in a list at the bottom of the **Find People** window.

List of Internet users with specified name

10 Click the **Web Site** button. Internet Explorer is opened, displaying the Switchboard Web Site. Feel free to browse the page and experiment with the Search tools.

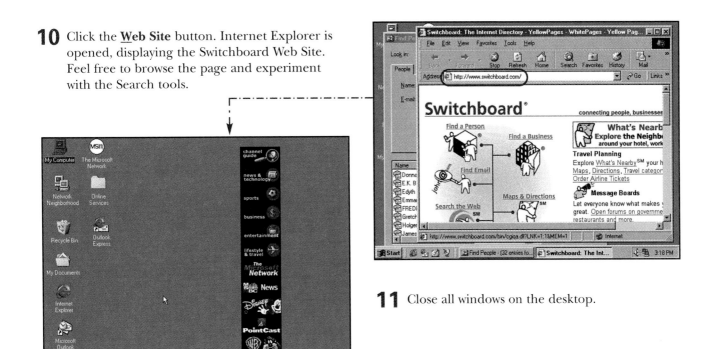

11 Close all windows on the desktop.

Task 3

Staying Up-to-Date with Channels

Why would I do this?

Internet Explorer contains a handy method for giving you up-to-date news and information on topics of your choice. This is accomplished through the use of *channels*. A channel is a special Web site designed to deliver Web content to your computer. A number of well-known news and information services maintain channels on a variety of topics. For instance, you can subscribe to the CNN channel for daily political news, the Wall Street Journal for business news, and ESPN for sports.

Most channel providers have new content daily. You can update your channels automatically so that all content is updated while you work on other projects or even at night while you sleep. Once updated, the channel can be viewed offline. In other words, you don't have to be connected to the Internet while viewing a channel. This technology is called *push technology* because instead of having to go search out information on the Web and pull it onto your computer, the information that you are interested in is automatically pushed onto your computer at a scheduled rate.

This lesson takes you on a tour of Internet Explorer Channels.

Channel Bar

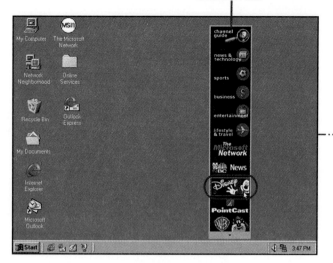

1 Click the **Disney** button on the Channel bar. If Disney has not yet been activated as a channel on your system, you will be shown an **Add Active Channel** button. Click the **Add Active Channel** button and work through the **Offline Favorite Wizard** setup process.

2 Internet Explorer opens on the desktop, displaying the Favorites list on the left and the Disney Channel on the right. Choose **Fullscreen** from Internet Explorer's **View** menu.

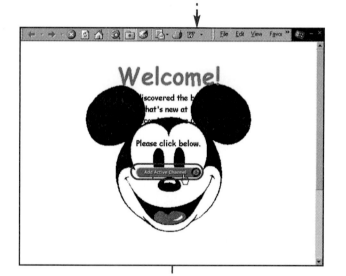

3 Fullscreen view allows you to use the entire display for the Web site. The Favorites list, Taskbar, and window borders are hidden to allow for the maximum view.

4 Explore the Disney channel. When done, move the mouse pointer to the left edge of the display to open the **Favorites** window.

> **In Depth:** The **Offline Favorite Wizard** will ask you about your Internet connection, if you'd like Web page links downloaded, and how you would like to synchronize the page. For now, you can just accept the default responses.

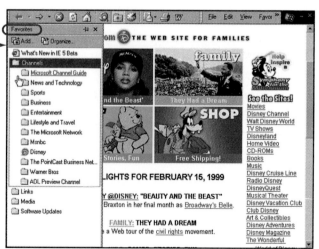

5 Open the **Channels** folder, and then choose **News and Technology** and **CNN Interactive**. **Add Active Channel** if it has not already been added.

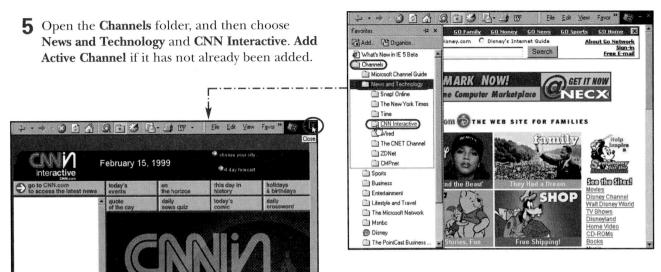

6 Explore CNN Interactive. When finished, close all windows on the desktop.

Task 4

Working with Active Desktop

Why would I do this?

Active Desktop allows you to add *Active Web Content* to your Windows 98 desktop. Active Web Content refers to items on your desktop that are updated each time you connect to the Internet, at chosen time intervals, or manually by clicking an Update icon. Microsoft offers a number of Active Desktop items that can be chosen from their gallery. These items include clocks, a stock ticker, weather maps, news headlines, and other items that are updated on demand and displayed on your desktop. Active Desktop offers yet another way to personalize your computing environment.

This lesson will show you how to add Active Web Content to your desktop.

1 Right-click the Windows 98 desktop. From the shortcut menu, choose **Active Desktop**, and then **Customize my Desktop**.

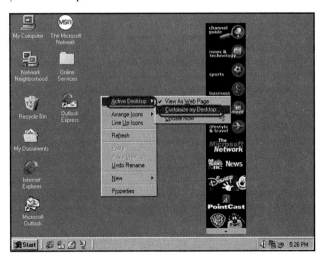

2 The Display Properties dialog box opens, displaying its Web desktop settings. Confirm that the **View my Active Desktop as a web page** option is checked and click the **New** button.

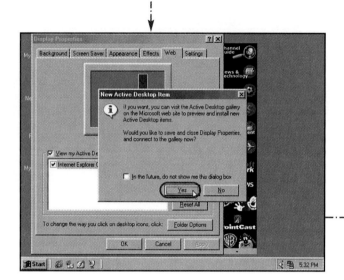

3 Confirm that you would like to connect to the Active Desktop gallery by clicking the **Yes** button.

4 Internet Explorer takes you to the **Active Desktop Gallery**. Close the **Favorites** window if it is still open from the last task. Maximize the **Internet Explorer** window. Your display should now look similar to the one in the following figure.

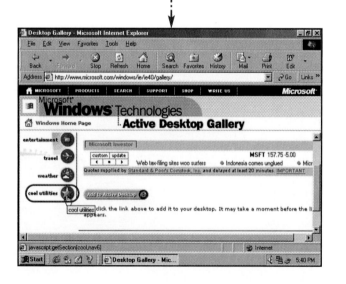

5 Scroll down the Web page and click the **cool utilities** icon.

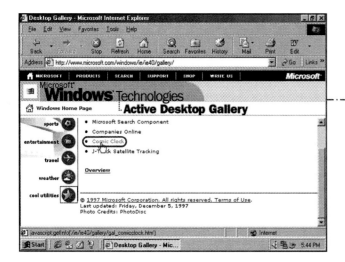

6 Click the **Comic Clock** link.

7 The Comic Clock is displayed on the Web page. Click the **Add to Active Desktop** icon to add it to your desktop. Click the **Yes** button for any confirmation boxes.

8 After a few minutes, the Comic Clock will be downloaded to your desktop. Close **Internet Explorer** to view the newly installed Active Desktop item. The Comic Clock delivers new humor to your desktop every time you click the **UPDATE** button (while you're connected to the Internet).

9 Right-click the desktop and choose **Active Desktop**. Then choose **Customize my Desktop** to return to the desktop Web settings page.

> **Quick Tip:** You can resize, move, or close Active Desktop items (including the channels bar) by pointing to the top edge of the window and using the title bar when it appears.

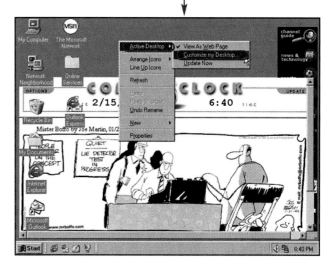

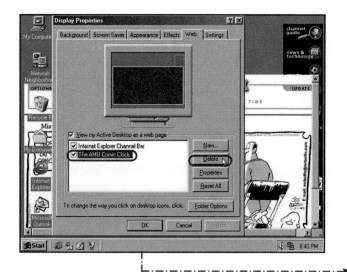

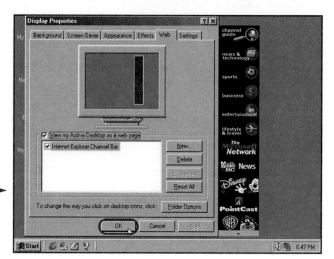

10 Select **The AMU Comic Clock** and click the **Delete** button to remove this item from your system. Click **Yes** in the Confirmation box.

11 Click **OK** to close the Display Properties window.

Task 5

Using Email with Outlook Express

Why would I do this?

Email is the most popular use of the Internet. It allows Internet users to communicate with each other almost instantaneously. The impact of email on social interaction is so drastic that it has been compared to the impact of the telephone. We can send an email message to other Internet users and have the message delivered seconds after it is sent. Messages can be sent to individuals or whole groups at a time. All kinds of files can be shared via email. The best part about it is that it's free!

This lesson will teach you how to use email with *Outlook Express*.

1 Click the **Outlook Express** button on the Quick Launch bar.

Pothole: If the Quick Launch bar does not appear on your taskbar, right-click an empty place on the taskbar, click Toolbars on the shortcut menu, and choose **Quick Launch**.

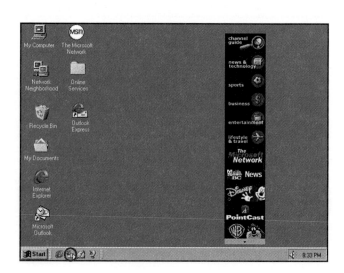

2 From the Outlook Express opening screen, click **Read Mail**. Work through the Setup Wizard, if presented.

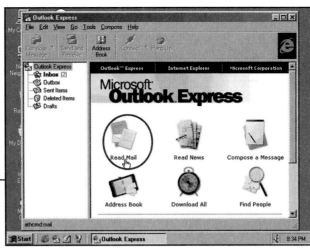

List of messages

Currently selected message

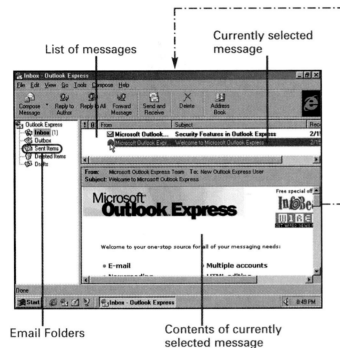

Email Folders

Contents of currently selected message

3 Maximize the **Outlook Express** window. The Outlook Express window is divided into three subwindows: a folders window, a listing of all messages in your mailbox, and the contents of the currently selected message.

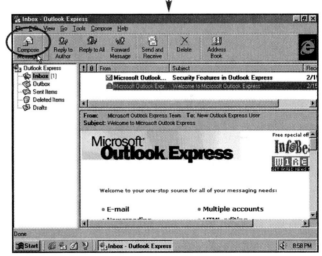

4 Click the **Compose Message** icon on the toolbar.

Pothole: You'll need to know some technical information concerning your *Email Server* in order to work through the Outlook Express setup wizard. You may need to get some assistance from your instructor or network administrator.

In Depth: Email folders are used to organize your email messages just as standard folders are used to organize files. You can create folders by choosing **Folder, New Folder** from the file menu. To move an email message to a folder, simply click and drag the message.

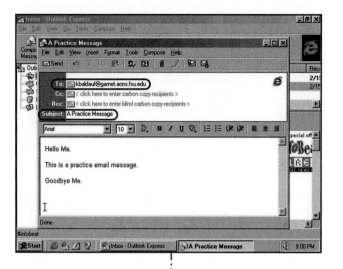

5 The New Message window is displayed. Type your own email address in the **To:** text box. In the **Subject:** text box, type **A Practice Message**. In the large text box, type the following:

Hello Me

This is a practice email message.

Goodbye Me.

Click the **Send** button on the toolbar.

6 The email is sent and the New Message window closes. Click the **Send and Receive** button on the toolbar. Outlook Express connects to your email server and downloads your new incoming email messages. If the email message to yourself is not downloaded, wait a couple of minutes and click the button again.

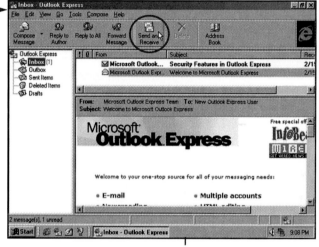

Quick Tip: Relate emotions in your email with *emoticons*— combinations of punctuation marks that when looked at with your head resting on your left shoulder resemble facial expressions. :-) (smile)

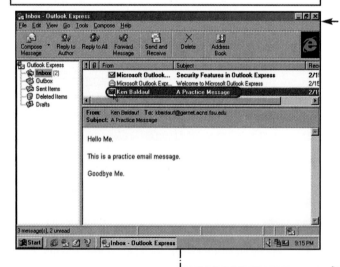

7 Select your message from your list of messages. The contents of the message are displayed in the Contents window.

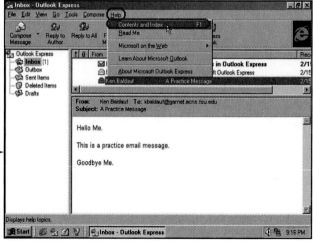

8 Open the Outlook Express **Help** menu and choose **Contents and Index**.

9 There's much that you can do with Outlook Express. Read through the Contents if you're interested in learning more. Close all the windows on the desktop.

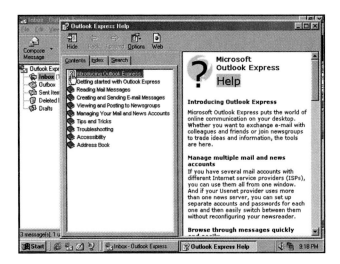

Task 6

Using Windows Update

Why would I do this?

When you purchase typical software, you purchase a static product, which is only as good as the current technology when it was created. Windows 98 differs in that it includes a feature that transforms the software into a dynamic product that can improve as technology improves. This feature is called **Windows Update**.

Windows Update connects your computer to the Microsoft Web site, where your Windows software is analyzed and updated to improved specifications. As this technology becomes more widespread, we will no longer need to purchase software in boxes.

This lesson will teach you how to use Windows Update.

1 Open the **Start menu** and click **Windows Update**.

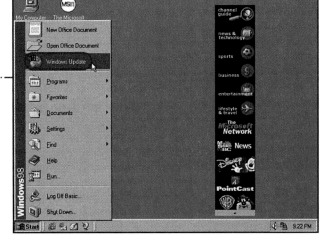

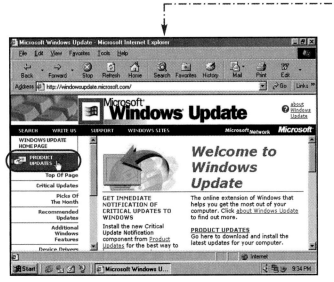

2 Internet Explorer opens to the Windows Update Web page. Click the **Product Updates** link.

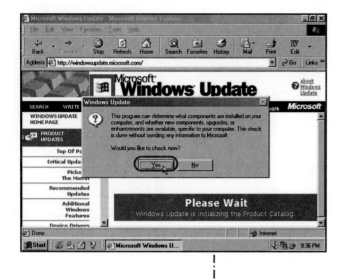

3 A confirmation box is displayed confirming that you would like Microsoft to check your system. Click **Yes**.

4 Your system is checked and you are presented with a list of available updated components. Items under the heading **Critical Updates** are very important to download, as they affect the safety and security of your system.

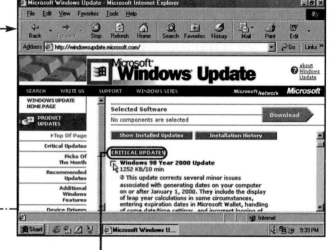

Critical Updates should be downloaded ASAP

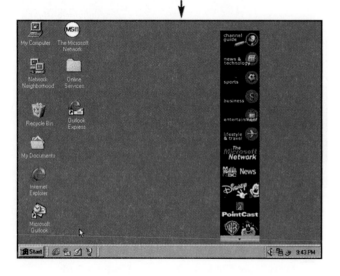

5 If you are working on your own computer, feel free to download updates at this time; otherwise, close all windows on the desktop. That's all for this lesson!

Student Exercises

True-False

For each of the following, circle either T or F to indicate whether the statement is true or false.

T   F   **1.** Networks are created so that computers can share resources.

T   F   **2.** Hyperlinks act to interconnect related Web pages.

T   F   **3.** Most Web page addresses begin with hppt://.

T   F   **4.** You can save your friends' email addresses in Internet Explorer's list of favorites.

T   F   **5.** You can search the Web on any keyword of your choice using a Search Engine.

T   F   **6.** Push Technology refers to the use of Web pages to push products on Internet users.

T   F   **7.** Channels allow you to view Web content offline (while not connected to the Internet).

T   F   **8.** Active Web Content refers to Web pages that include moving graphics.

T   F   **9.** Email is the most popular use of the Internet.

T   F   **10.** Windows Update allows you to update your Windows 98 software.

Identifying Parts of the Windows 98 Screen

Refer to the figure and identify the numbered parts of the screen. Write the letter of the correct label in the space next to the number.

1. _____
2. _____
3. _____
4. _____
5. _____
6. _____
7. _____
8. _____
9. _____

A. URL

B. Return to previous Web page

C. Content of selected email message

D. Channel bar

E. Email folders

F. Links

G. List of email

H. Quick Launch bar

I. List of favorite Web pages

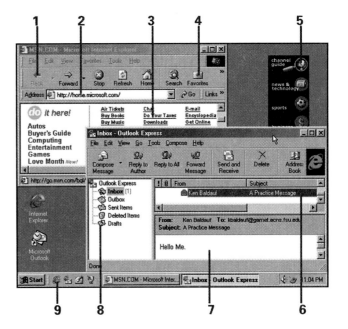

Matching

Match the statements below to the word or phrase that is the best match from the list. Write the letter of the matching word or phrase in the space provided next to the number.

1. ___ A collection of computers that are connected together to share software and hardware resources.

2. ___ The largest of all interconnected networks.

3. ___ A graphical user interface which uses convenient methods for accessing Internet resources.

4. ___ Internet files designed to be viewed with a Web browser.

5. ___ A computer program that allows you to view Web Pages.

6. ___ Marked text within a Web page that, when clicked, opens a related Web page.

7. ___ A Web page address, beginning with http://.

8. ___ A special Web site designed to deliver Web content to your computer.

9. ___ A Web tool used to perform keyword searches of the Web.

10. ___ The network computer that is responsible for controlling your email service.

A. Network

B. The Internet

C. The Web

D. Web Page

E. Web Browser

F. Hyperlink

G. URL

H. Channel

I. Search Engine

J. Email Server

Reinforcement Exercises

These exercises are designed to reinforce the skills you have learned by applying them to a new situation. Detailed instructions are provided along with a figure where appropriate, to illustrate the final result. The exercises that follow should be completed sequentially. Leave the workbook open at the end of each exercise for use in the next exercise until you are specifically directed to close it.

Exercise 1

1. Open Internet Explorer.

2. Go to **www.cnet.com**.

3. Explore the CNET Web site.

4. Go to **www.hotwired.com**.

5. Explore the HotWired Web site.

6. Go to **www.mtv.com**.

7. Explore the MTV Web site.

8. Use the **Back** and **Forward** buttons to navigate through pages that you've visited.

9. Choose one or more of these sites and add it to your **Favorites** list.

10. Use the **History** button to return to the CNET Web site.

11. Close **Internet Explorer**.

Exercise 2

1. From the Start menu, choose **Find** and **On the Internet**.

2. Do a web search on the keyword **Jokes**.

3. Browse through the resulting pages for a laugh.

4. From the **Start** menu, choose **Find, People**.

5. Use the Yahoo People Search to search for a friend on the Internet.

6. Close **People Search** and **Internet Explorer**.

Exercise 4

1. Right-click the desktop, choose **Active Desktop** and **Customize my Desktop**.

2. Deactivate any active desktop items currently being used by clicking the check box to remove the checkmark.

3. Click the **New** button to open the **Active Desktop Gallery**.

4. Browse through the gallery and find an Active Desktop item that you like. Click the **Add to Active Desktop** button.

5. Close Internet Explorer and go back to the **Customize my Desktop** screen.

6. Return your desktop to its previous settings.

Exercise 3

1. Click the **MSNBC** button on the Channel bar.

2. Change the Internet Explorer view to FullScreen.

3. Add **MSNBC** as an active channel on your system.

4. Browse through the MSNBC channel.

5. Close **Internet Explorer** and **Channels**.

Exercise 5

1. Open **Outlook Express**.

2. Click the **Compose a Message** option.

3. Email a message to a classmate or friend and place your own email address in the cc: box so that a copy is sent to you.

4. Click the **Download All** option from the Outlook Express main window.

5. Click the **Read Mail** option from the Outlook Express main window.

6. Check for your email message in the list.

7. Highlight the message and press Del to remove it.

8. Click the **Sent Items** folder in the list on the left. This displays all of the messages that you've sent.

9. Go back to the main menu by clicking **Outlook Express** at the top of the list of folders on the left.

10. Close **Outlook Express**.

Lesson 9
Customizing Windows 98

Introduction

To make Windows 98 a more personal and useful place for you to work, Microsoft has made it easy for you to customize it. You can adjust desktop settings to suit your working style. Using the World Wide Web from Windows 98 is easy and entertaining. Microsoft has integrated its Web browser, Internet Explorer, into Windows 98 so that it is just as easy to explore the Web as it is to explore your desktop.

In this lesson, you learn to open the *Control Panel* and use it to change a variety of Windows 98 settings. You learn to change the date and time, alter the desktop wallpaper pattern, add and delete programs from the Start menu, and set a screen saver.

Visual Summary

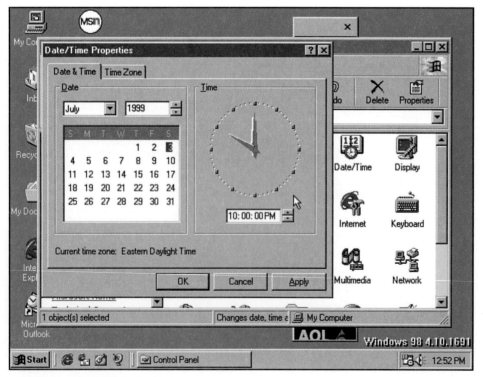

When you are done with Task 2, you will have a Windows 98 desktop that looks like this:

Task 1

Opening the Control Panel Window

Why would I do this?

The Control Panel contains many settings that you use to modify your Windows environment. You can personalize the Windows environment to suit your individual operational needs.

In this task, you learn how to open the Control Panel window from My Computer, as well as from the Start menu.

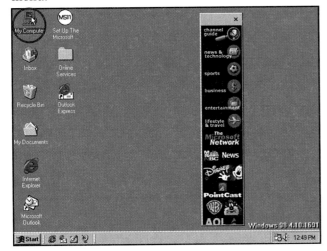

1 Open the **My Computer** window.

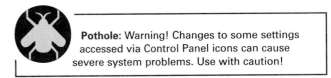

Pothole: Warning! Changes to some settings accessed via Control Panel icons can cause severe system problems. Use with caution!

2 Double-click the **Control Panel** folder. The Control Panel window opens.

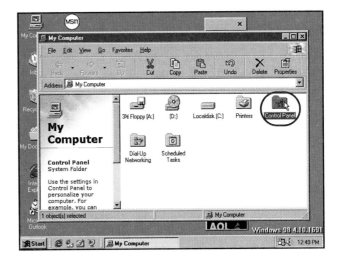

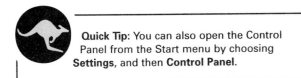

Quick Tip: You can also open the Control Panel from the Start menu by choosing **Settings**, and then **Control Panel**.

Pothole: Some network administrators prefer to deny users access to the Control Panel in order to ensure system security. If you are unable to access the Control Panel, check with your instructor on how to proceed or skip ahead to Task 5.

Task 2

Changing the Date and Time Settings

Why would I do this?

Your computer places a time and date stamp on every file you save, thus identifying it for use later. If your system clock is wrong, this feature ceases to be useful. Change your system's date and time when your computer lists the wrong date or time on the taskbar.

In this task, you learn how to change the date and time settings from the Control Panel window.

1 If necessary, open the **Control Panel** window. Double-click the **Date/Time** icon. The **Date/Time Properties** dialog box opens. If necessary, click the **Date & Time** tab to select it.

> You can also change the date and time settings by double-clicking the time area on the extreme right of the taskbar. This also opens the Date/Time Properties dialog box. Windows 98 automatically adjusts the date and time for your computer to accommodate daylight savings time and leap years.

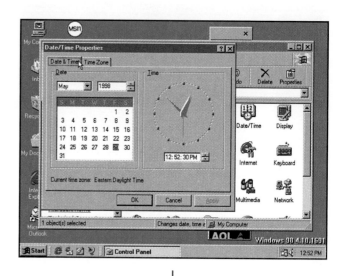

2 Click the list arrow next to the month in the Date area of the dialog box. Click **July** from the list, then click **3** on the calendar to select the day.

3 Click the list arrow next to the year until it reads **1999**.

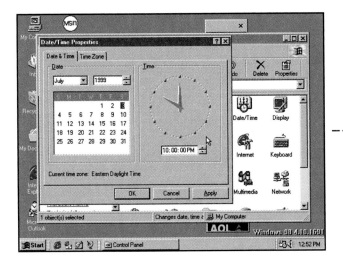

4 In the **Time** area of the dialog box, double-click the hour and enter 10, double-click the minutes and enter 00, doulbe-click the seconds and enter 00 and click the up or down arrow to change the time to 10:00 PM.

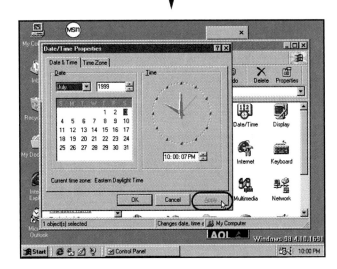

5 Click **Cancel** to exit the Date and Time settings without making any change.

Task 3

Changing the Wallpaper on Your Desktop

Why would I do this?

You can modify the desktop in Windows by changing its background, or *wallpaper*, to make your work area more of a reflection of your personality. Windows offers such intriguing wallpaper patterns as Clouds, Bubbles, Stitches, and Waves, among others. Choose any of these as a background for your desktop, or choose none, whichever you prefer.

In this task, you learn how to add a pattern to the background of your desktop window.

1 In the Control Panel window, double-click the **Display** icon. The Display Properties dialog box opens. If necessary, click the **Background** tab.

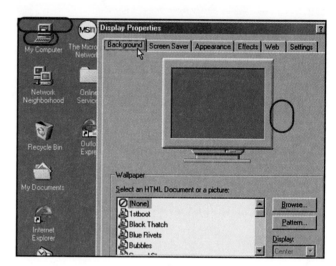

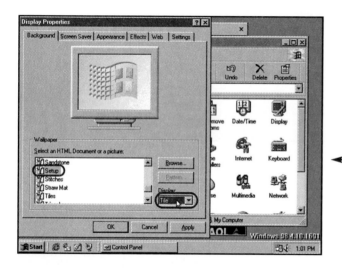

2 In the Wallpaper area of the dialog box, click **Setup** by. The wallpaper is previewed in the window.

Pothole: If the wallpaper selection Setup is not available, select another pattern or wallpaper of your choice.

Task 4

Using a Screen Saver

Why would I do this?

When you use Windows or Windows applications, the concentration of bright or white colors on the video display can, over a period of time, burn into the screen. When you turn your computer off, you may see a "ghost" of the Windows screen on the display. A *screen saver*, or moving pattern, can help save your screen from this burn-in effect by displaying a pattern whenever your computer is on but not in use.

In this task, you learn how to apply a screen saver to the video display.

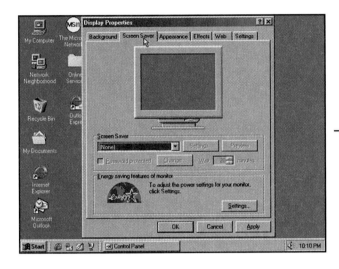

1 If necessary, open the **Control Panel** window and double-click the **Display** icon. The Display Properties dialog box opens. Choose the **Screen Saver** tab.

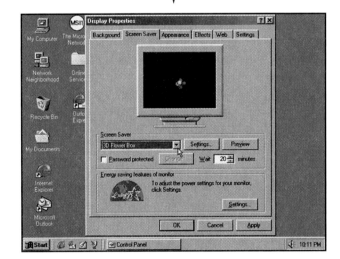

2 In the Screen Saver area of the dialog box, click the drop down list arrow and click **3D Flower Box** (The screen saver pattern is previewed within the Display Properties window.)

Pothole: Since your computer may be configured differently, you may have a different number of screen saver selections. If 3D Flower Box is not a screen saver selection, pick any other one from the list.

Quick Tip: If you click the **Preview** button immediately after you select your screen saver, the screen saver will be shown on the full screen. It will be removed from the screen when you press a key on the keyboard or when you move the mouse.

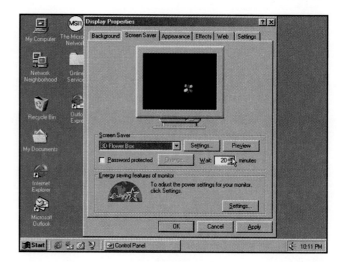

3 In the **Wait** text box, click the list arrow and select **20** as the number of minutes to wait before the screen saver starts. In this example, if the keyboard or mouse is not touched for more than 20 minutes, the screen saver goes into effect and stays in effect until you touch the mouse or use the keyboard. Click **Cancel** to exit Display Properties without applying the changes.

Task 5

Adding Programs to the Start Menu

Why would I do this?

You can add programs to the Start menu to make it more convenient to use. For example, you may want to add programs that you use often to the Start menu so that you can access them more quickly.

In this task, you learn how to add a program to your Start menu.

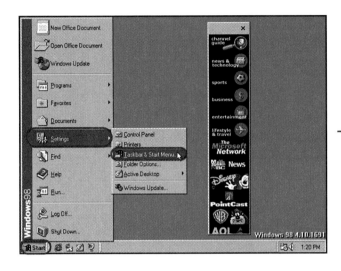

1 If necessary, close all open windows. Make sure that the Learn Windows 98 CD is in the CD-ROM drive. Click the **Start** button on the toolbar and choose **Settings**, **Taskbar & Start Menu**.

2 The **Taskbar Properties** dialog box opens. Click the **Start Menu Programs** tab.

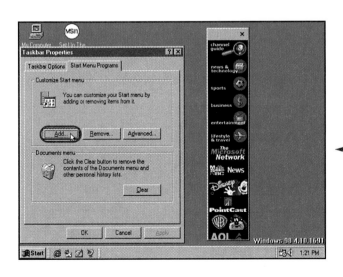

3 In the Customize Start Menu area of the dialog box, click the **Add** button. The Create Shortcut dialog box opens.

4 Click the **Browse** button and then, from the **Look in** list box, choose the CD-ROM drive location. Double-click the **Student** folder to view its contents.

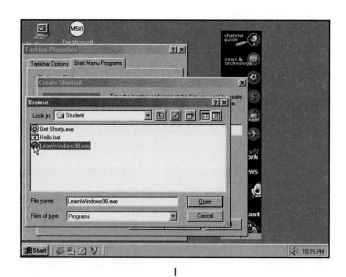

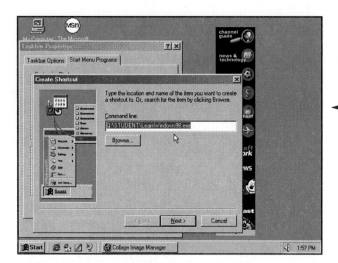

5 Double-click the **LearnWindows98** program in the dialog box. You will automatically return to the Create Shortcut dialog box. Notice that the program title shows in the text box.

6 Click **Next**. The **Select Program Folder** dialog box opens. If necessary, click **Programs** in the **Select folder to place shortcut in** area of the dialog box.

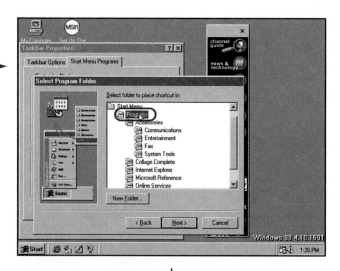

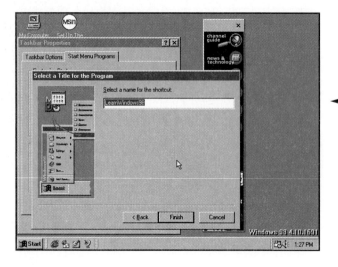

7 Click **Next**. The program is placed in the Programs folder and the **Select a Title for the Program** dialog box opens. Click Finish.

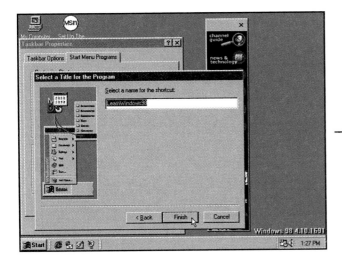

8 From the Taskbar Properties dialog box, click **OK**.

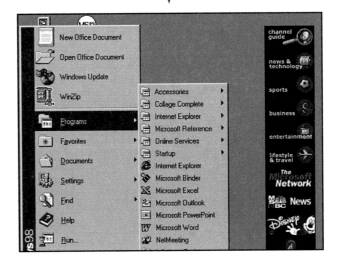

9 From the Start menu, choose **Programs**, **LearnWindows98**. The newly added program is *launched*. When you are done working with the program (its instructions are self-explanatory), click the **End This Program** button.

Task 6

Deleting Items from the Start Menu

Why would I do this?

Just as you may want to add programs to the Programs menu, you may want to remove them when they are no longer useful.

In this task, you learn how to quickly remove a program from the Programs menu. However, it is recommended that you exercise caution when deleting programs so you do not mistakenly delete the wrong program.

1 On the taskbar, click the **Start** button, then select **Settings**, then **Taskbar & Start Menu**.

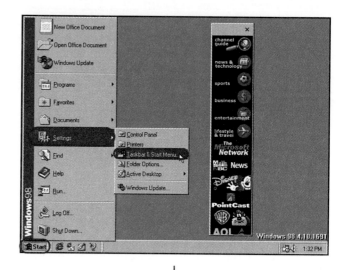

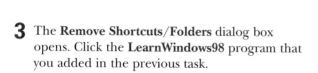

2 From the **Taskbar Properties** dialog box, make sure that the **Start Menu Programs** tab is selected and click the **Remove** button.

3 The **Remove Shortcuts/Folders** dialog box opens. Click the **LearnWindows98** program that you added in the previous task.

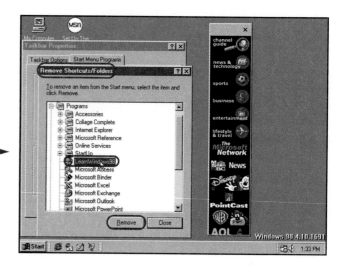

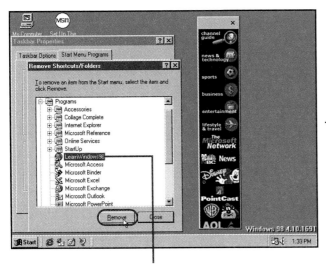

Program icon will be
erased from menu

4 Click the **Remove** button on the Remove
Shortcuts/Folders dialog box. The program icon
is erased from the menu, but the program is not
erased from the disk.

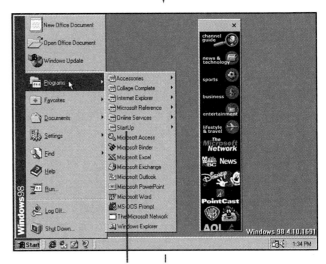

Program icon is deleted from the
Programs menu

5 Click the **Close** button to return to the Taskbar
Properties dialog box. Close the Taskbar
Properties dialog box. From the Start menu,
click **Programs**. Notice that the Learn Windows
98 program icon has been deleted.

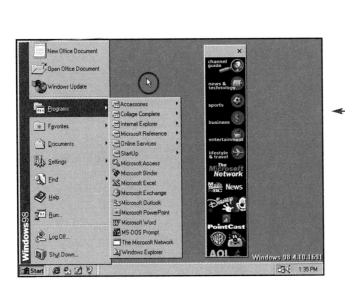

6 Click any blank area on the desktop to close the
menu.

Student Exercises

True-False

For each of the following, check T or F to indicate whether the statement is true or false.

T   F   **1.** Programs may be added to the Start menu via the Settings command on the Start menu.

T   F   **2.** Windows 98 allows the user to change the time and date settings.

T   F   **3.** Shortcuts can be created for programs, files, or folders.

T   F   **4.** Launching a program means to delete it.

T   F   **5.** Most system settings can be accessed through items in the Programs menu.

T   F   **6.** The desktop background is called its wallpaper.

T   F   **7.** A screen saver is interrupted by moving the mouse.

T   F   **8.** It would be a wise idea to set a screen saver to go into effect after five seconds of inactivity.

T   F   **9.** Control Panel icons should be accessed with caution.

T   F   **10.** Copying an object is the same as creating a shortcut.

Identifying Parts of the Windows 98 Screen

Refer to the figure and identify the numbered parts of the screen. Write the letter of the correct label in the space next to the number.

1. _____
2. _____
3. _____
4. _____
5. _____

A. Preview window

B. Power-saving settings

C. System setting icons

D. System Time settings

E. Background and Screen saver settings

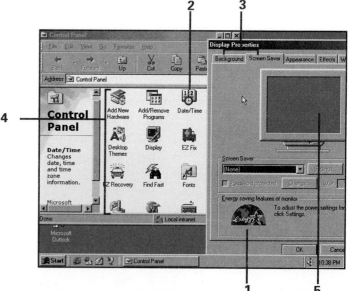

Matching

Match the statements below to the word or phrase that is the best match from the list. Write the letter of the matching word or phrase in the space provided next to the number.

1. ___ All system settings can be accessed from this window.

2. ___ A wallpaper design that is repeated across the desktop uses this option.

3. ___ The Control Panel is accessed through this Start menu command.

4. ___ Other than using the Control Panel or the Settings command, the date and time can be set by double-clicking the date and time on this object.

5. ___ You can change your desktop color from this window.

6. ___ Open this windows when you want to add items to the Start menu.

7. ___ Brighten up your desktop with this feature.

8. ___ In addition to using the Start menu, the Control Panel can be opened from here.

9. ___ This feature entertains while you are inactive.

10. ___ Hold the mouse pointer on this object and the date will be displayed.

A. Taskbar

B. Display Properties

C. Screen Saver

D. Wallpaper

E. Clock

F. Tiled

G. Taskbar Properties

H. My Computer

I. Settings

J. Control Panel

Reinforcement Exercises

Exercise 1

1. Change the settings of the wallpaper to a design of your choice. Then change them back to their original settings.

2. Check your system's date and time. If they are not correct, adjust them so they are correct.

Exercise 3

1. Delete the **Get Shorty** program from the Programs menu.

Exercise 2

1. Add the **Get Shorty** program on the Learn Windows 98 CD to the Programs menu.

2. Run the **Get Shorty** program from the Start menu.

Glossary

ActiveMovie Control   A multimedia accessory that provides both audio and video features.

Active Window   The window in use when other windows are open.

Address Bar   Located directly below the Standard Buttons in a window. It permits you to type in a location on your computer or on the Web to go to. You also can pull down a list of locations to go to.

Automatic Word Wrap   A feature in WordPad (and other word processors) that automatically moves text to the next line when the current line is full.

Bitmap   A type of graphics file; for example, a wallpaper file called circles.bmp is a bitmap file.

Browser   Also known as a Web browser. Software used to access and navigate through Web pages. Internet Explorer is the Web browser that comes with Windows 98.

Cascade   A windows arrangement in which each window is successively placed behind other windows.

Channel Bar   An object on the Windows 98 desktop that gives you quick access to your favorite and the most popular Web content on the Internet.

Check Box   A list of choices in a dialog box that a user can select. Check boxes are not mutually exclusive.

Check Mark   A mark placed in a check box to indicate the box has been selected.

Clicking   A single click to a mouse button.

Clipboard   A holding area where data is placed when it is cut or copied from an application.

Contents Help   A help feature that lets the user select from a range of topics to narrow down to the topic that he or she wants to find help on.

Control Menu   It is accessed by clicking the icon on the upper-left corner in the title bar of a window. It contains menu commands to Restore, Move, Size, Minimize, Maximize, and Close the window.

Control Panel   The place where your computer's settings, such as those for the time, date, and video display can be changed.

Copying   1) The duplication of a source disk to a destination disk. 2) Placing a copy of selected text or an object on the Clipboard.

Cursor   When pasting into a WordPad document, the cursor indicates the place where the data will be pasted.

Cutting   Removing a selected object or text from an application and placing it on the Clipboard.

Desktop   In Windows 98, any part of the computer screen viewing area is known as the desktop.

Dialog box   A window that requires input or a response from the user.

Double-click   Two rapid clicks to a mouse button without moving the mouse.

Drag-and-Drop   A feature that lets you move an object from one location by grabbing it with the mouse, dragging it to a new location, and dropping it there.

Dragging   Holding down the left mouse button on an object and moving it.

Embed   When you embed an object into another object, you can edit the embedded object by double-clicking. The toolbars and menus from the embedded object's application are used to edit it.

Find Help   A Help feature that permits the user to enter the topic on which he or she needs to find help.

Folder   An icon that represents the place where data, programs, or other folders are stored.

Formatting   The preparation of a disk for use on a PC.

Hypertext   Text that, when clicked, links to another related topic or shows related information on the object that was clicked.

Icon   A picture that represents an on-screen object, such as a program, window, or Web page.

Index Help   This Help feature presents all Help topics in alphabetical order and lets you type in a topic to search for help.

Keyboard shortcut   A combination of the (Alt) key and another key used to substitute a mouse action. For example, pressing the (Alt)+(F) key is a keyboard shortcut for clicking the File menu.

Launch   To execute or run an application.

Link or Hyperlink   An object you can click on that jumps you to another location. Usually, the mouse pointer changes to a picture of a hand when it is placed on a link.

List box   A box that presents the user with a list of choices to select from.

Logical View   A view of objects represented as icons.

MS-DOS   A text-based interface and operating system that preceded Windows 98. In general, commands are entered via the keyboard as opposed to pointing and clicking with the mouse.

Maximize Button   Enlarges a window to fill the desktop.

Media Player   An accessory used to play multimedia files.

Menu   A list of choices displayed on the screen from which the user may select.

Menu bar   A horizontal bar that appears across the top of a window that shows different menu choices.

Minimize Button   Reduces the window to a button on the taskbar.

Mouse   A small, hand-held input device that is equipped with one, two, or three control buttons. It is used to control one's position on the desktop and to manipulate objects on the desktop.

Mouse Pointer   The onscreen pointer that is controlled by moving the mouse.

Multimedia   The combination of text, graphics, audio, or video in a PC presentation.

Online Help   Help that comes integrated with the software itself instead of in separate printed instruction manuals.

Option button   A list of choices from which a user can select. Option buttons are mutually exclusive.

Page   Because Windows 98 displays a window's contents as it would an Internet Web page, the contents of a window is sometimes referred to as a page.

Paint   An application that is used to create and edit graphic images.

Pasting   Placing an object from the Clipboard into an application.

Physical View   A view of objects represented in a hierarchical structure.

Pointing   Placing the mouse pointer on an object.

Progress bar   An object usually found in a dialog box that indicates the progress of an action while it is being completed.

Prompt   A signal from the computer indicating that it is ready to receive input from the user.

Recycle Bin   A place for storing files when they are deleted from the hard drive. Files may be permanently deleted from the disk by emptying the Recycle Bin.

Restore Button   Restores a window to its previous size.

Start Button   The button used to open the Start menu.

ScanDisk   An application that can detect and repair some disk errors.

Screen Saver   An image that is displayed on the screen after a certain period of inactivity that prevents screen burn-in.

ScreenTip   A small box containing the name or some information about an object that is being pointed to with the mouse pointer.

Scroll Bars   An object used to move part of a window into view when it is too small to display all of its contents.

Shortcut   An easily-accessed icon that is created by the user to represent a commonly used object.

Shortcut menu   A menu that may be conveniently accessed by pressing the right mouse button on an object.

Smart Toolbar   On Internet Explorer, the toolbar recognizes if you are on a Web page, or in files and folders. The buttons on the toolbar change accordingly.

Standard Buttons   Located below the menu bar on a window, the Standard Buttons permit you to work with a window much like you would work with Web pages on the Internet.

Start Menu   A list of program names that appears when you click the Start button.

Submenu   A menu that opens as a result of the mouse being placed on another menu command.

Tab   Within a single dialog box, there may be more than one page or view. The different views or pages can be accessed by clicking a tab.

Taskbar   A bar, usually located on the bottom of the Windows 98 screen. It includes the Start button as well as the status of other windows programs.

Text box   An area in which the user enters text or numbers.

Tiling   Displaying open windows in equal size.

Title Bar   The top part of a window containing the Windows icon, file name, minimize, maximize, restore, and close buttons.

Toolbar   A toolbar that appears immediately under the menu bar. It contains navigation and editing buttons.

Toolbar   A collection of buttons or other objects that appear on a window that provides a shortcut in place of accessing menu commands.

URL   An acronym for uniform resource locator. In short, a Web address such as www.yahoo.com.

Wallpaper   An image on the screen that acts as a background on the desktop.

Windows Explorer   A program used to view and manage folders and files.

WordPad   An accessory used to create and edit unsophisticated documents.

Index

A

Save As, 36
shortcut key
combinations,
25
Shut Down
Windows, 12
Taskbar Properties,
133
disk errors and
ScanDisk, 86
disks, formatting, 26-27
Display Properties
dialog box (Internet
Explorer), 116
displaying Favorites
list (Internet
Explorer), 109
documents
opening, 4
saving, 36
DOS applications
running, 38-39
using in Windows,
40-41
double-clicking with
mouse, 4
downloading Comic
Clock to Active
Desktop, 117-118
dragging with mouse, 4
dropping and dragging
files and folders, 52

E

Edit menu commands
Paste, 97
Select All, 95
Undo, 79
editing
embedded
data, 101
graphics with
Paint, 79-81
text with WordPad,
77-78

email, 118-120
embedded data,
editing, 101
emoticons, 120
establishing Internet
connection, 107
executing DOS
applications, 38-41
exercises, 123-125
exiting
applications, 34
windows, 11

F

F1 key (context-sensitive
help), 70
Favorites button,
Internet Explorer, 109
File menu commands
Close, 11
Format, 27
Save, 37
Save As, 36, 47
files
copying, 49-50
deleting, 54-55
dropping and
dragging, 52
finding, 52-53
moving, 51-52
naming, 46
saving, 34, 36,
46-48
storing in
folders, 44
viewing, 55-56
Find All Files dialog box,
52-53
Find command (Start
menu), 52
Internet Explorer,
110
Find Help features,
65-66

Find People dialog
box, 112
finding
files, 52-56
Quick Launch bar,
118-119
Web sites, 110-113
floppy disks, 86
Folder Options dialog
box, 25
folders
creating, 45-46
deleting, 54-55
description of, 33
dropping and
dragging, 52
email, creating, 119
finding, 52-53
My Documents,
uses of, 37
naming, 46
opening, 4
overview of, 44
renaming, 46
saving files to,
46-48
Format command (File
menu), 27
Format dialog box, 27
formatting
disks, 26-27
text, 96
Forward button,
using, 24
Fullscreen command
(Internet Explorer),
114

G-H

graphics, creating and
editing, 79-81
hand position for using
mouse, 3

hard drive errors and
ScanDisk, 86
Help features
Contents, 61-63
Find, 65-66
Index, 63-64
overview of, 60
Web Help, 71-72
What's This?, 69-70
Help topics, printing,
67-68
Help Topics dialog box
Contents tab, 62-63
Index tab, 63-64
opening, 61
Search tab, 65-66
hyperlinks, 62, 107,
110-113

I-J

icons, 3, 45
Index Help features,
63-64
Internet
Active Web
Content,
115-118
connecting to, 107
email, 118-119
hyperlinks, 107
push technology,
113
searching, 110-113
Web sites
channels,
113-115
CNET, 108
locating, 108
WWW (World
Wide Web)
accessing, 107
push
technology,
113
URLs, 107

Folder Options, 25

Large Icons, 20

viewing

Favorites list
(Internet
Explorer), 109

files, Windows
Explorer, 55-56

W-Z

wallpaper on desktop,
changing with
Control Panel, 130

Web Help feature, 71-72

Web browsers, 107-108

Web sites

channels, 113-115

CNET, 108

locating, 108

What's This? Help
feature, 69-70

wildcard characters,
finding files using, 53

windows

arranging on
desktop, 20-21

changing displays,
18-20

closing, 11

minimizing, 7

moving, 9

opening, 4, 6-7, 17

Outlook Express,
119

restoring, 8

sizing, 9

title bars, 8-9

Windows Explorer, 55-56

Windows Update,
121-122

WordPad

closing, 34

opening, 33

using, 77-78

writing text (WordPad),
77-78

WWW (World
Wide Web)

accessing, 107

push technology,
113

URLs (Uniform
Resource
Locators), 107